G000160401

THE
MEMORY BE GREEN

AN ORAL HISTORY OF A DEVON VILLAGE

By the same author

FEVER: A STORY FROM A DEVON CHURCHYARD

THE
MEMORY BE GREEN

AN ORAL HISTORY OF A DEVON VILLAGE

Liz Shakespeare

LETTERBOX BOOKS

First published 1990
by
Letterbox Books
Littleham
Bideford
Devon
EX39 5HW
Reprinted 2006

For information on other books by
Liz Shakespeare and ordering details, go to
www.lizshakespeare.co.uk

Copyright © Liz Shakespeare 1990
All rights reserved

ISBN 0 9516879 0 5
978-0-9516879-0-1

Printed and bound by SRP Ltd, Exeter

Foreword to the 2006 Edition

Rural life has continued to change since this book was first published in 1990. The influx of people escaping from urban areas has continued, bringing with them different ideas and expectations. Agriculture has experienced a period of crisis and in many areas it is only the specialist or very large farms which survive. House prices have risen dramatically, distorting the balance of social classes in villages.

However it is perhaps a matter of "Plus ça change, plus c'est la même chose". In Littleham, on which this book is focused, the sense of community is, if anything, stronger than it was sixteen years ago. In a recent parish survey most people highlighted friendly neighbours and a vibrant community as central to their enjoyment of the village. Local organisations thrive and new clubs and societies are being formed. There is much that the people who were interviewed for this book would recognise.

The elderly people I interviewed are no longer with us; however, many lived to be well into their nineties and enjoyed the degree of local fame they experienced by having their names in print. Alan Marshall and Lionel Badcock, both names synonymous with Littleham, have sadly also died. But all their memories, now becoming ever more distant, serve to remind us of earlier times and it is their past which informs our future.

Liz Shakespeare. December 2006.

Dedicated to Annie Palmer.
"The memory be green."
(*Hamlet. Act 1. Scene ii. 2*)

Acknowledgements

I would like to thank the following people for giving so freely of their time and their enthusiasm: Maud, Lionel and Aileen Badcock; Gwen Barrow; Gertie Beer; Horace Beer; Sylvia and Raymond Clements; Charlie Cook; Fred; Winifred Johns; Alan Marshall; Vi McDougall; Margaret Smale; William.

I am grateful to everyone who loaned old photographs and to the North Devon Record Office for access to Littleham School records and copies of the Bideford Gazette.

Special thanks to Chris, Camilla and David for their time and expertise.

Cover illustration by Chris Collingwood

Cover design by Camilla Palmer

Present day photographs by David Beadle

Contents

Chapter One	First Impressions	page	1
Chapter Two	Friends and Neighbours		6
Chapter Three	Signposts to the Past		10
Chapter Four	The Changing Village		15
Chapter Five	Gertie Beer		19
Chapter Six	The Pride of the Housewife		24
Chapter Seven	The Big House		31
Chapter Eight	Charlie Cook		39
Chapter Nine	A Pattern of Work		44
Chapter Ten	Farming		48
Chapter Eleven	The Farmer's Wife: Annie Palmer		58
Chapter Twelve	Journeys and Diversions		65
Chapter Thirteen	A Sense of Community		72
Chapter Fourteen	The Village School		84
Chapter Fifteen	Lanes and Dwellings		95
Chapter Sixteen	The Village Today		105

Chapter One

First Impressions

It was ten years ago on a dull, cold October day that I first saw Littleham. I had driven from London through Hampshire, Wiltshire and Somerset. The motorway came to an end and I crossed the border into Devon. Almost immediately the roads narrowed and the countryside changed, a view of rolling hills, pockets of oak woodland, low white farmhouses huddled amongst barns in narrow valleys. I passed through the market towns of South Molton, Barnstaple and Bideford, so quiet, so unchanging I might have been not just miles but years from the frenzy of London.

I saw the signpost and turned up a very narrow winding lane between massive hedgebanks. I met another car, bonnet to bonnet on a sharp right-angled bend and reversed to let it pass, the driver waved as though he recognized me. The lane wound past two or three houses until a sign told me I was in Littleham although there was no village in sight. The hedgebanks continued, interrupted now and then by gates which showed glimpses of small fields and more hedges; I passed a few more houses without gaining any impression of size, whether they were old or new. Then the hedgebanks came to an end and my view widened. On my right was a row of old cottages, small, low, all painted white or near white perhaps and seeming to blend one into another. I stopped and got out of the car. Everything seemed small and close, the cottages close to each other, close to the lane, the windows small and close making me feel conspicuous as I stood there in the road. Afterwards I could remember little of the external appearance of the cottages, only this impression of proximity, like a stranger's face which comes too near.

I recognized one of the cottages from the photograph I had pored over and knocked at the door. Inside the room was small, long and low, the ceiling brought even lower by the beams which ran across its width. The room was dominated by a huge stone fireplace which formed one of the end walls, the fire which blazed in it lit that end of the room, lit the face of a small child asleep on a narrow window seat. I tried many times in the weeks that followed to remember the details of that and the other three rooms but the concentrated politeness called for when talking with a stranger had made it difficult to take in more than an impression. I only remembered the smallness, the nearness of everything which was emphasised by the large furniture, the narrow stairs and low doorways. Yet the impressions I retained were enough to make me feel that this was where I wanted to live. Fortunately my husband felt the same and within a few months the cottage was ours.

At first we reluctantly continued to live in London, making occasional weekend visits to Devon to redecorate the cottage and keep the garden in order. Each time we visited I discovered features that I had not noticed before. The small opening at the side of the fireplace which led into the huge bread oven, shaped like a beehive and big enough for a child to climb into. The ceiling beam in the centre of the room which was newer than the others, did this suggest the previous existence of a wall there I wondered, dividing the room into two smaller ones with a central passage? A deep mysterious cupboard next to the fireplace at ceiling height from which a difference in the quality of the air, a slight breeze could be detected. I imagined that I was the first to have noticed these things, as though the cottage was somehow a natural thing which had grown without help from human hand.

As winter turned to spring the intense green of new growth appeared in the garden where there had been bare earth and developing leaf buds gave promise of shade and seclusion in the summer. And it was so quiet. As a contrast to the belligerent clamour of inner city schools, the traffic which never stopped, the alarms, the sirens, all the sounds of stress and aggression, as a contrast to this the silence here in this garden was almost a physical presence. I started to count the weeks, then the days.

At this time, in the early days, I was hardly aware of the village. We had bought a house and as I saw nothing which displeased me in its surroundings I took very little notice and was content at first to look no further than our cottage and our garden. It was only when I finally moved in and started to explore the area on foot that I began to notice where I was living. Although I had had a vague wish to live in a small community I had very little idea of what that might entail or whether indeed the scattered houses which made up the village formed any sort of community. Littleham did not conform to the idea most people have of a village, certainly not the city-dwellers ideal of thatched cottages clustered round a village green. It did not seem to have a centre, or at least none that was apparent to the outsider.

There were four roads which met in a crossroads which I later learnt to call Crossways after the house and garden which occupied one corner. Like the rest of the village, this was situated on the side of a hill with a sweeping view of small wooded valleys leading to further hills patterned with a kaleidoscope of fields in every shade of green and brown; on a clear day the hazy mass of Dartmoor was visible on the horizon. This crossroads might have been expected to form the centre or at least a focal point, a meeting place. But there was nothing there except a few houses and a lay-by where there were usually a few cars parked. Three of these roads, or lanes perhaps as all were barely wide enough for two cars to pass, led out of the village, two of them winding towards other villages a few miles away and the third to Bideford, the market town where I was brought up.

The fourth also appeared to leave the village behind as after the small cluster of cottages and one or two bungalows the lane was again bordered by high hedgebanks. After a short distance there was a collection of dilapidated farm buildings, some of concrete blocks and corrugated iron and on the other side of the road one or two of cob, the earth and straw walls now exposed to the wind and rain and in danger of becoming eroded. Brown bad-smelling water dripped from the jagged edge of a rusty iron chute protruding from the bank and fell on to the long fresh grass beneath; deep ruts at the side of the road showed where tractors drew up to fill muck-spreaders from the slurry pit. Opposite was a Methodist chapel, a low white-washed building with arched windows and a steeply sloping roof edged with ornate ridge tiles. A low stone wall ran around the front of the building, broken by a wrought iron gate which led to the pitched entrance porch.

The lane wound up a hill past more fields hidden by high hedges. On the right was a phone box set back from the road in a lay-by which bore a warning sign, "Devon County Council. Passing Place Only." It seemed unlikely that the order would ever be enforced and indeed there were usually one or two cars parked there. From here the row of cottages, the row of which our cottage was part, could be seen a little further up the lane, a long low terrace. At first I only noticed our own house, studying it as I walked up the road until every detail became familiar and comfortable. It was some time before I started to look at the other cottages and noticed where one finished and another began, saw the little differences which gave each its own character. One or two had been modernised, reroofed with asbestos slates and the tiny bedroom windows replaced by dormer windows. The cottages at the beginning of the row had three or sometimes four steps leading to the front door through very narrow front gardens which were divided from the road by stone walls, there was just room for a small flower border where campanula, antirrhinums and red valerian grew. Further down the row, which I later saw to be two terraces with a narrow drive to a garage in between, further down the gardens were a little bigger allowing tiny lawns, a few shrubs and even in one case, a cherry tree. It took me some time to see these things. Not liking to stand and stare at my neighbours' houses, I had to be content with quick glances as I walked past. It was longer still before I learnt who lived in each cottage.

At the end of the row of cottages the lane forked, running each side of a small field which formed a triangle. The right fork ran past two farmhouses both of which had signs on their gates so I was able to call them by their correct names from the start, Higher Boundstone and Nether Boundstone. The first appeared empty although tractors still drove in and out of its yard and there was a barn full of fresh hay. After a while I realized from the over-loaded cars which arrived at the farmhouse from time to time that it was let to weekly summer visitors, the farmer having built a modern house elsewhere in the village. The second house was beautifully kept, its flower-filled borders and immaculate paintwork suggesting that it was no longer owned by a working farmer. A row of chicken houses like Army Nissan huts were the only reminder of its original purpose.

After passing a small overgrown pond the lane narrowed until it was barely wide enough for one car. An old signpost announced the way to the church, a necessity as the village was now left behind and it was unlikely that a visitor seeking the church should try such a narrow overgrown lane. This soon became a favourite walk. The church was built like the rest of the village on the side of a hill but being in a slight hollow and on the very edge of the village, a quarter of a mile indeed from the nearest houses, it only became visible when the lane suddenly emerged from the high overgrown hedges and opened into a wide sweep. The church stood small and rugged, changeless as Stonehenge, dwarfing the headstones which gathered around it. The voices of jackdaws rang out from the bell-tower where they were building their nests. On the far side of the churchyard a footpath which I discovered from the ordnance survey map led past the old Rectory and down into the woods.

If I took the left fork after the row of cottages I passed a field on each side, again giving the impression that the village was left behind. Then there were some more houses, a semi-detached pair of council houses, one or two bungalows with very large tidy gardens, the lawn edges kept short and straight. One had plaster gnomes strategically placed around the garden and a plastic heron next to a fishpond. Then more fields, a large dilapidated Victorian building which appeared to house chickens, one or two more houses and a farm surrounded by huge stone barns and marked by a helpful sign which told me it was Apps Farm. Finally the sign which marked the village boundary. But still there was one more building, the village hall, incongruously outside the village itself and half a mile from where most people lived. It was a long low building which had the appearance of having been constructed from odds and ends and rooms added when the need arose. It had an air of desolation and it wasn't until I saw the large car park full of cars one night that I realised it was still used.

This then was Littleham as I first became aware of it, a collection of buildings set in some of the most beautiful scenery in England. It was not a village to attract tourists, being set apart from main roads and having little to recommend it other than the little church hidden amongst the trees and its sweeping views of fields and hills. The web of hidden lives and shared memories which made up the life of the village did not reveal itself to the casual eye.

Chapter Two

Friends and Neighbours

When we first moved into our cottage I imagined that people already living in the village barely noticed that it had been sold and were unaware that it was empty for some months. I took little interest in my neighbours, seeing no further than my own house and garden and assuming that they took no interest in me but as the details of my surroundings became familiar I started to notice the people around me. It was then that I realized I had been under scrutiny all along. When meeting my neighbours over the garden wall or in the lane outside the cottages and introducing myself, I found they already knew my name, knew where I had come from, what work I did, knew my maiden name and who my mother was. This made early conversations rather unsettling, I felt at a disadvantage and did not like to ask questions when there was no need for them to be reciprocated. Having been born and brought up in North Devon, a member of a family well known among the older farming community, I was accepted by the locals but seven years in London had made me feel an outsider. Everyone seemed to know so much about the village and I so little that after each brief conversation I was left in a state of confusion with so many new names and places to assimilate.

It was Jean I got to know first, a woman of indeterminate age with short steel grey hair and strong kind features. She lived alone in a cottage larger than mine which I later learnt had been converted from two some years before, one of which had had only one room up and one down. She had moved to Littleham "from away" as the local expression went, to be away from the bustle of towns and traffic and she seemed to revel in her solitude. She was one of the few people who lived happily in the village without a car, relying on the weekly bus service and occasional lifts from friends for shopping. I would hear her talking in her deep calm voice to her Great Dane bitch and the pet rabbits which hopped about at liberty in her garden. Our gardens were divided by a stone wall which stood at chest height. Small trees, cherry, apple and buddleia growing on each side helped to make the gardens secluded but it was still possible to see into the other garden when standing close to the wall. We both valued our privacy and would call out a greeting before approaching the wall to talk, in the same way as one would knock at a door before entering.

On the other side of our garden was a tall privet hedge so it was a little longer before I got to know my neighbours well. Margaret and Reg and their two grown up children had lived in the village all their lives. Even in the early days when I found it difficult to put names to faces and remember where people lived, I never forgot Margaret and Reg. They weighed perhaps forty stone between them, something which they bore with great good humour. I rarely heard anything through the thick walls which divided our cottages but occasionally, when the cars of visiting relations were parked outside their house, I would hear as from a great distance the sound of deep roars of laughter interspersed with the higher almost hysterical laughter of the women.

Reg worked as a driver for North Devon Farmers, delivering sacks of grain and fertiliser. I once saw him loading his lorry outside the depot in Bideford and he hoisted the heavy sacks on to his immense shoulders as if they weighed nothing at all. In the evenings he would stand at his garden gate with his arms folded on the gate post, talking to passers by and I would hear his great ringing laugh. If I came outside my cottage he would boom out a greeting, "All right then?", always more of an exclamation than a question. Sometimes I would see him driving his lorry when I was out in my car and, unable to shout, he would flash his lights and a huge hand would wave from the window.

On warm evenings, when Reg was outside his cottage leaning on his gate post, other people would gather to talk and Margaret would come out to join them. It seemed that some were just passing although I never knew where they had come from or where they were going, there were few people to be seen walking their dogs in those early days. Some like Glennie came particularly to talk. At that time when I knew so few people, it was easy to remember Glennie. Whenever it was fine he could be seen somewhere in the village, sitting in his wheelchair at Crossways or toiling up the hill towards the cottages, his muscular arms urging the wheels on. He would stop outside Margaret and Reg's or continue to the end of the row and park his wheelchair in the road where the lane forked down to the church. He would then sit, his chin dropped on to his chest and his mouth open a little. He rarely caused an obstruction here as an hour might pass before a car came along and he would then rouse himself and direct it around his wheelchair with a flourish and a grin.

Glennie was usually to be seen somewhere in the village so I would pass him on my walks but I soon learnt that conversation with him was difficult. Accustomed to local dialect as I was, his speech was thickened by more than accent and the stutters and half-formed words were slurred into an almost unrecognisable language. However I would stop and make some comment about the weather and I would usually make out a few words forced out with great effort amongst the jumble of sounds and stammers. After a while I found these words were the same whatever I said to him. "Well. Me dear. As a matter of fact. To tell the truth. I've been thinking." When he'd finished he would slap his knee and let out a great roar of mirth but I never did learn what he'd been thinking.

Among the group which gathered outside the cottage next door to me on warm evenings was a dark haired, middle-aged woman who lived somewhere on the road to the village hall. I was not sure of her name and did not always recognize her when she walked past my cottage, indeed she seemed to look different each time I saw her. Sometimes she would be wearing a faded flowered apron which gave her a plump appearance and slippers which caused her to drag her feet a little. At other times she would be wearing heels which tapped on the road as she walked past. Always she walked with the slow easy confidence of one completely at ease in her surroundings, so different from the tense hurried gait of the city dweller who is wary of appearing curious and keeps her eyes on the ground ahead. I used to wonder where she was going, there was no shop in the village to visit and on the whole people were not in the habit of walking for the pleasure of it. It was some weeks before I realized that there were in fact three dark-haired middle-aged women all living near each other on the road to the village hall. I gradually learnt their names but it was a long time before I was able to put the correct name to the face reliably. By the time I knew where each of them lived we had had many conversations together and this early confusion was forgotten.

Sometimes I would arrive home in my car when Reg and Margaret were standing by the gate in their little front garden talking to one of the dark-haired women and perhaps someone else whose face was half-familiar to me. As I got out of the car Reg would roar out his greeting and the others smile encouragingly so I would go over to join them. I would then be aware of a lull in the conversation as they tried to accommodate me. Having known each other for so many years they had no need for explanations and talked in a form of shorthand which was difficult for the outsider to follow, containing as it did many oblique references to past events and unknown people. I always found people very willing to answer my questions about the village or about themselves but these conversations always felt rather one-sided as the questions were rarely reciprocated. Contrary to popular opinion there did not appear to be a penchant for gossip in the village, perhaps discussion was unnecessary because everyone was so well known. I was never asked questions about myself and if I talked about my plans or my past in an effort to be open, this was received with some embarrassment as if the listener might appear prying merely through hearing what I was saying. So conversations progressed with many smiles and much goodwill but I learnt more of the village through looking around me than I did from my neighbours.

I could be sure to see Glennie when walking through the village, sitting in his wheelchair where he could see the occasional tractor or car pass by and where he could hear a friendly word from all who passed him. When he sat outside the end cottage where the lane forked down to Church Lane he could usually rely on the company of another man. John lived in this end cottage with his wife Rene. He had recently retired from his job as driver for a local builder's merchants and spent much of his time leaning on his gate or standing in the lane with his arms folded on his ample stomach gazing out over the fields and woods which lay below his cottage. He told me about his past employment and how he sometimes worked for a local farmer, driving a tractor or harvesting potatoes. On this occasion he was genial and expansive, winking at me as he laughed at something funny which had happened to him. But when I passed his cottage the very next day he remained at his gate, his hands thrust into the bib of his dungarees and his face stonily impassive, deliberately determined not to meet my eyes. The first time this happened I tried to recall our conversation, wondering what I had said to upset him but then found him as friendly as before when I next passed. I found out after a while that everyone experienced his moods occasionally and I learnt to watch his eyes before I called out a greeting so that I might know whether it would be reciprocated. As time passed his moodiness diminished and we became great friends.

After a while I got to know who lived in each of the cottages and was able to match names to faces reliably, knowing also a little of the history of each family, how long they had lived in the village and where they went to work. But it was a lot longer before I came to understand the web of relationships and social gatherings which made up the community life of the village. To the outsider it seemed a village where nothing happened; arrangements for meetings and social events were made largely by word of mouth and took place quietly in private houses or set away from the village itself in the village hall. It was not until I read a report in the local paper that I knew that Littleham was home to one of the best skittle teams in North Devon. Tucked away from main roads, the village seemed to hide itself from the public eye and continued in its daily round as if immune to the changes that took place in the world outside.

Chapter Three

Signposts to the Past

The village hall was built at the end of a ridge. It was an exposed spot on a windy day, not a place where I felt inclined to linger, but when the sun shone and the air was stirred by a light breeze I often stopped to gaze at the panorama of rolling hills which stretched in every direction, studded occasionally with the gleaming white oblong of a farmhouse. There were two ways to reach the village hall. I could walk down the narrow winding lane to the church, I called this way Church Lane and later found that this was the name by which it was generally known. Having passed through the churchyard, which resembled a meadow of flowering grasses and wild flowers rather than a burial ground, I reached a stony track. If I turned right I came to the footpath which led down past the old Rectory and into the woods. Turning left I followed the stony track, an old cart track, up between low hedges bordering two fields which that first year were sown with barley. Once I heard the rattling song of a corn bunting, briefly, for the first and only time in the village. At the summit of the low hill the track emerged opposite the village hall.

If I went the other, more direct way I left my cottage and walked straight through the village ignoring the right turn to Church Lane. This took me past the bungalows with their large tidy lawns, past the derelict Victorian building with its smell of chickens, past Apps Farm on the left with its huge stone barns. The village hall stood on an unmarked crossroads formed by the lane from the village, the stony track down to the church, and two other lanes. One of these led up to the next ridge which it then followed in an unusually straight manner for a Devon lane before winding down to the Torridge valley. Until I knew better I called it Long Lane. The fourth lane was called Scratchyface, something I must have learnt very early on as I never gave it a name of my own.

At the junction to Scratchyface a sign leaning drunkenly to one side declared, D.C.C. Unsuitable For Heavy Traffic. I passed a pair of red-brick semi-detached cottages on my right, there were chickens pecking at the foot of the hedges and they scattered, panic stricken as I approached. Two goats tethered in a paddock lifted their heads and bleated before continuing with their grazing. The lane wound gently down, the view to either side obscured by the massive hedgebanks which loomed high above my head. The leaves had turned colour now and the tiny stream which ran on one side of the lane was hidden here and there by drifts of brown and gold torn from the trees in recent high winds. After a while the hedge on my right dipped to reveal a small rough field strewn with clumps of brambles, bereft now of blackberries. Beyond the field stood a very large brick built house, made up of a jumble of parts and added wings and surmounted by countless tall chimneys. Although obviously a house of some importance there seemed to be no grand entrance, merely a rather rusty iron gate which looked as if it would be stiff on its hinges, leading to a muddy track.

The lane ran down so steeply now as it plunged towards the valley that I could understand how it came to be called Scratchyface. The stream had gushed across the road during recent heavy rain and had left stones strewn on the surface so that it resembled a river bed more than a highway, and indeed few cars tackled the steep gradient. A gateway, disused now and overgrown with brambles gave a sudden view of the valley below and the River Yeo, tributary of the Torridge, winding through low meadows. In front of the greenly wooded slopes on the far side of the valley a buzzard drifted idly then rose slowly, circling, its brown and cream wing patterns showing now against the clouded sky as it soared upwards. I picked a ball of dried grass from the hedgebank and tossed it idly in the air before noticing its strange weight; pulling it gently apart I found a tiny reddish-brown dormouse curled in a ball with its paws covering its face and its furry tail twisted over its shoulder. It was breathing visibly, not yet in deep hibernation. I covered it up carefully and replaced it in the hedge, hoping I had not disturbed it too much.

All my walks around the village were marked by discoveries. Every day I found something new, something obscured from the casual eye and I imagined then that I was the only one who knew about these secluded places and hidden evidence. I was not yet part of the village community and the memories of the past which, had I but known it, were still so vivid to many people, could not be shared with me. Unaware then of these collective memories, I assumed the knowledge of the past to be dead, only to be found by careful searching. Daily I walked in the narrow winding lanes between the dense hedges, past the houses both old and new; daily I looked out over the distant hills with their patchwork of fields and woods reaching as far as the shadowy view of Dartmoor; the solitude of the walks, the emptiness of the lanes made me believe I was seeing things long forgotten.

It was the wells I noticed first. Walking one day on the stony track on the far side of the church I saw an arch of stone set low in the hedgebank. Overgrown with ivy it was easily overlooked, but closer examination revealed a hood of stone curving protectively over a shallow depression. In the interests of safety the well had been filled in but there was still a smell of cool damp earth and ferns grew in perpetual shadow on the rear wall. After that I searched for more wells. Some in secluded places remained as they had always been, the ivy a little thicker perhaps, the stone crumbling a little here and there but down the cool, dark tunnel of stone the glint of water could still be seen. Some had been fitted with small wooden padlocked doors opening on to the road to keep curious children away from the dangerous fascination of those chilly depths. I studied the ordnance survey map and found there to be about fifteen wells marked in the village. Most were set into hedgebanks but a few were to be found in the middle of fields and these were still in use. They were usually covered with a heavy stone lid and water was hauled up in a bucket on a rope and poured into an old bath for livestock. The clothes of the farmworker, jeans, check shirt, had changed but the movements, the hauling on the rope, the braced legs, were the same as they would always have been a hundred, two hundred years ago when the drawing of water was a familiar and wearisome activity to everyone in the village.

The lanes were quiet and I seldom saw a car when I was walking. I could hear the sound of a car or tractor engine a quarter of a mile away and as it approached I stood back in the hedge to let it pass; always the driver would wave and sometimes stop to talk. But there were other lanes which no car ever used, some were overgrown and barely wide enough for the walker, others were occasionally used by tractors to reach fields distant from the metalled roads. These tracks were rough underfoot, some strewn with loose stones and some thick with mud in winter, churned up by the horses which occasionally passed that way. One steep stony track led from the road I called Long Lane down between high hedges which in early summer bore a profusion of bluebells, red campion and cow parsley. The lane fell steeply for half a mile until it reached an old mill and then a metalled road which led to the River Torridge and on into Bideford. It was clear that this was the most direct way into the town, superceded now by the longer but easier route along Long Lane, or Wagon Road as I later learnt to call it. Walking down this abandoned road, away from traffic noise and with only the mewing of buzzards to be heard, it was easy to imagine oneself in an earlier time when wheeled transport was only available to the wealthy and people were often to be seen toiling up the hill with their baskets of produce from the market.

The signposts to the past could be found through careful searching but the signposts of the present were less obvious. Signs are needed to direct the stranger to his destination and inform him of local amenities and tradesmen, noticeboards to inform inhabitants of forthcoming events; in a village away from the tourist routes, where the few people to visit were regulars and where events in the village were communicated by word of mouth, signs and notices were considered superfluous. This sometimes made things difficult for the newcomer to the village.

The postal address of the row of cottages where I lived was Mount Pleasant but there was no sign to declare this and few of the cottages bore a number on their doors. In any case this name was rarely used locally, the cottages being known simply as "the Village". This led to some confusion until I realized the significance of the term as I would be informed by someone I knew for certain to live just fifty yards down the road that they too used to live in "the village". One or two of the cottages bore names on their front walls but more were known by names which related to their present or previous occupants, so there was Jean's Cottage, John's, Granny's Cottage which was sometimes referred to as "Granny's Cottage as was" to indicate to a newcomer that the lady in question had now passed on. I had no such memories to identify my own cottage and felt the need give it a name; when the sign appeared it caused much interest and some surprise, I felt the same sense of mild indignation when years later other houses in the village were renamed in defiance of tradition.

On the road below Crossways which I had learnt to call Littleham Hill was a modern house of unusual design which boasted a familiar red and gold sign in the front garden declaring a post office. It bore so little resemblance to any other post office I had ever known that I used to wonder whether the sign was some sort of practical joke designed to tease strangers in the village and indeed I never saw anyone enter the house when I passed it on my walks. If it was indeed the post office, should one walk up to the front door and ring the bell or walk straight in? I was afraid that should I do the latter I would find myself walking into the owner's sitting room so I continued to buy my stamps elsewhere and the mystery was not solved until the house was sold and the sign appeared outside a different, more approachable house in the village.

Other signs were equally enigmatic. A little way above the post office the Crealock Arms was announced at the end of a lane. The lane led past a private house and a small field where curious bullocks romped over to the fence, it came to an end at a farmhouse next to a small pond containing half a dozen sleepy ducks. There was no sign of a pub and it was not until later that I learnt that the farmhouse was indeed the Crealock Arms converted a few years before, the village having been without a pub for some fifty years. I was told that the village possessed another amenity, a weekly bus to Bideford. Where this elusive bus stopped and when one might hope to see it remained a mystery as there was no bus shelter or timetable to be seen. Had I dared to enter the post office it may be that I would have found out such things.

There were indications that the village had once been the scene of greater activity than I found it to be. There was the Old Forge, the Old Rectory, Hoops Cottage which had once been Hoop Inn and later when the fashion for naming caught on, the Old Post Office and the Old School. There were still tradesmen in the village but it was some time before I learnt of them as the builders and decorators had no need to advertise, finding their custom among their friends in the community. There was a yard and two very large sheds which bore a profusion of signs including advertisements for brake fluid, a warning to beware of cats and dogs and a smaller one which declared the premises to be Smales Garage but I never saw any evidence of activity outside. Next to one of the council houses nearer my cottage was another collection of sheds and here there was usually a tractor or Landrover and one or two cars being worked on. A friendly old man was often to be seen working in the garden, he would wave and call out a greeting and it was not long before his son was servicing my car along with others in the village. In such a small close knit community it was essential to have human contacts to find out more about the village.

Chapter Four

The Changing Village

It seemed an unchanging village; the ancient fields and hedges, the farms regulated by tradition, the quiet lives lived behind closed doors, the slow repetitive cycle of growth and decay, all combined to give the appearance of permanance. But there were changes, invisible at first to a stranger's eye. It might be days or weeks before I heard of a death, or the birth of a new baby. A particular walk not undertaken for some while might reveal a tree blown down in a storm, a new barn erected. A house was sold, another reroofed, an old outhouse was knocked down and a greenhouse erected in its place. The changes which seemed so new to me were part of a continuous process.

It was not long after I moved into my cottage that the new building started. There had of course been new houses built in the last few years but to me they were now part of the established village, I had never seen the fields where there were now lawns and garages, as a child I had never played in the stream which now ran underground. So for me it was a shock to see an excavator in the lane near my cottage one morning, desecrating the village that had so recently become familiar. I had picked blackberries from the hedgebank that was now being gouged out and dumped into a waiting lorry, I had looked forward to seeing primroses peeping from a myriad shades of green in the coming spring. I would have to look elsewhere, it was not long before two, then three houses stood where cows had grazed and the lush hedgebank was replaced by low stone walls and wrought iron gates.

It wasn't until the post office moved that I began to feel a part of the community. The modern house which I had never dared to enter was put up for sale and for a few months the village was without a post office. I learnt, not immediately but only when it seemed to be common knowledge, that Margaret was applying to run the post office in the cottage next to mine and before long a new exterior door and alarm system was installed, the dining room converted and Margaret was rather nervously selling her first stamps. Now the lane outside my cottage became busier with customers passing to and fro to the post office and I would hear the shop bell ring from my garden. It seemed to me to be busier than the modern house, I had never seen anyone enter there as I passed by on my walks through the village, no doubt many people were reassured by the fact that Margaret came from an old Littleham family and was very well known and liked. Whatever the reason the post office soon became the new heart of the village and I began to meet more of my neighbours and to make friends.

It was not until my second year in the village that I began to look forward to the annual events that formed a large part of village life. The first village fete I went to soon after I moved to the village was, unusually, on a wet day. It had rained all morning and I had stayed at home, oblivious of the work going on at the village hall where stalls were reluctantly being set up indoors, the dripping bunting festooned across the lane and signs erected on the main roads from Bideford. I wandered along in the afternoon to have a look and it seemed a half-hearted affair. I waded through a gateway of thick mud into a wet field where a few old cars were displayed and some strange disembodied engines chugged steadily beside their owners. In the hall were a few desultory stalls manned by bored attendants, roll a penny, children's lucky dip, a bottle stall. To a stranger such as I it seemed a dull affair.

By the following year my husband was on the village hall committee, I was running a stall myself and we knew about the months of preparation which took place before the event, making it the largest and most popular fete in the area. When I saw all the added attractions which brought so many people I realized that it had been all but cancelled the previous year. There was maypole dancing, a brass band, a gymnastic display, gymkhana, dog show and of course the teas which had become quite famous for their quality and value for money, coaches were provided to transport people to and from Bideford. The fete still is the high spot of the village year, an occasion for hard work for the villagers but also much enjoyment and an opportunity to swell village hall funds.

The stationary engines which I had first seen at the fete soon after my arrival reappear every year. Some people own just one, others have collected numerous examples of various ages and conditions, the interest obviously having spread from one person to another until now I can't help wondering whether Littleham owns a higher percentage of stationary engines per head of population than any other village. As well as the village fete the engines are displayed at car and traction engine rallies, the larger rallies providing the venue for an annual holiday for several families who arrive with their caravans, tents and the trailors bearing the precious stationary engine, two journeys often being necessary to transport everything. These events are as important to many in the village as the fete, an opportunity to get away from familiar surroundings and patterns of work without leaving friends and neighbours behind, many more villagers visit the rallies for the day so that it sometimes seems as if the population has moved en masse to a new site.

The fete and the traction engine rallies were the big events of the summer. They were remembered in the autumn when there was a film show at the village hall showing cine films taken that summer, one or two of the stationary engine owners being also the proud owners of cine cameras. The hall was always full on this occasion and the films of brightly coloured traction engines chugging around a field watched with polite interest; the real enthusiasm was saved for appearances by familiar faces when a roar would go up from the audience, "There's Fred!" and poor Fred would cover his face with his hand and laugh, embarrassed but proud.

Also in the autumn was the firework display organised by the village hall committee for local children and the Christmas sale of work held to raise money for the church. Then there were the regular events, the bingo, the skittles, the Women's Institute. As more houses were built more children moved into the village, there having been a lull in the birth rate for a few years in the manner of small communities. Now there were enough small children again to start a weekly mother and toddler group which helped to diminish the isolation felt by women new to motherhood and the village.

Changes in the village began to take place more quickly now. The field at the end of the row of cottages was sold for building and after a winter of excavators, builders' lorries and mud there were eleven more houses in Mount Pleasant. The new houses were numbered clearly for all to see. The Victorian building housing chickens which I had learnt to be the former school was renovated. A garden was sold for building, then another. Farmhouses were sold, the barns converted and the land taken to enlarge other farms. Margaret and Reg closed the post office and moved into Bideford, they were followed by others who had lived all their lives in the village. Apps Farm was sold and work started on converting the huge stone barns which had formerly housed a slaughterhouse and, before that, a brewery. Signs sprung up throughout the village informing the newcomers of the public footpaths and events at the village hall. Every week new estate agents' boards appeared.

The film show no longer takes place but the fete, the rallies, the bingo and the skittles, the W.I. and the toddler group, the Christmas sale, the fireworks, they are still popular. There is now also a thriving youth club which for two years has produced an impressive annual show and has organised dances to raise money which have been attended by many people in the village. Village life thrives, or does it? As I look around at any village event I see many familiar faces, people who have lived in the village far longer than I, many of them all their lives. Some have now moved out of the village to neighbouring towns but return frequently, some weekly, still feeling their roots to be in the village. There are also some less familiar faces, people who have recently moved into the village and want to be part of the community, a few help to organise events and have new ideas about how things should be run. But what of the others? There are many who have moved into the village who are only seen in their cars as they drive to and fro from their houses. Their work, their entertainment and their friends are in the towns and they have no need for the village community. Houses are bought and resold before their owners' faces have become familiar. If this is to be the pattern for the future can the village survive as a community?

The past that I know is slipping away. What of the village of earlier times? As people move away, their children unable to pay the high prices asked for houses, as others die, early memories of the village die with them. What was it like to live in the village before cars opened up new possibilities, before running water and electricity made life easy, before television kept people shut in their own homes? I resolved to find out more about the past before it was too late.

Chapter Five

Gertie Beer

The nearest farm to my cottage is Boundstone Farm. The centre of the biggest farm in the area, the farmhouse itself is now let to summer visitors and the farmer and his family live in a newer house elsewhere in the village. It is a large squarish house with additions to the original structure and is only visible from the road leading to the church, being shielded from the village by a stone wall and a row of tall conifers. Now that it does not have permanant occupants it is sometimes forgotten by the rest of the village and few people have reason to call there but it is not many years since the house was the centre of great activity. I had learnt that the farm had been in the Stevens family for several generations but it was not until I started to enquire about older people who used to live in the village that I learnt about Gertie Beer, born at Boundstone Farm and now in her ninetieth year.

I visited Mrs Beer at her bungalow where she lives alone in a pleasant neighbourhood a few miles from the village. She was expecting me and I saw her at the window as I opened the wrought iron gate and walked through a well-tended garden to the front door. I was welcomed by a small, plump, smartly dressed woman looking far younger than her years. She was eager to talk of her memories of the village at the beginning of the century and as she invited me into her sitting room she immediately started telling me about the busy life she remembered.

"The hard work there used to be for the farmers and their helpers! And the people in the village, they used to have to fetch every drop of water, what a job it was, it's a miracle how we survived it all! And now we've got everything useful and convenient! People worked hard to rear their children and in the village they had to fetch every drop of water and quite a little distance from their houses, you wonder now however they managed it! Must have been dreadful really, yet for all they were always generous people, ready to help others and worked hard for their family you know, marvellous how they got on really. And when they growed up they all married somebody you know, quite respectable and nice people." It was significant that it was the work of water-fetching that Mrs Beer remembered first, I was to learn later that this was central to the memories of many people in the village. She talked very quickly as the memories came flooding back, pausing only for a chuckle and quite unperturbed by the presence of my tape recorder.

"I was born at Higher Boundstone, 1900, quite a good while ago now! Stevens was my maiden name. I'm the oldest, course years ago they had such long families, that made it harder for everybody didn't it? Things have got more modernised now and they carry on a bit easier than they used to, good job too! I had six brothers and two sisters. I lost my mother when I was nine year old and my father married again, Miss Alice Vanstone from Putford, she was wonderful really to take on six of us children, she did her very best for us in the cicumstances and soon got us all more comfortable and made us feel life was worth living again. She had three of her own children and brought us all up happy together.

My dear old father didn't live all that old, sixty five when he died, 1932. He had double pneumonia and he was never quite the same after. It made things very hard and they had a lot of bad luck too, I know one year he lost an awful lot of sheep, lambs and that, one year he lost his favourite horse. I can remember my parents both shedding tears once, all the things that seemed to be going wrong. Yet for all they were good living people and Christian like. When Father died my brothers carried on with the farm because they was all growing up, they used to do what they could, they were in their teens then I reckon.

He was a wonderful Christian man, he wouldn't have nothing but the Bible on the table Sundays, he wouldn't like us to read a newspaper, he wouldn't allow that sort of thing. We used to have to do so much on Sundays, milk of course, but it was almost wrong to go to the garden for vegetables Sundays, especially among the older people. I wasn't very struck with dances and Father and Mother didn't care for us going to them, they used to think that was too worldly I think! We were Methodists but Father used to go to church sometimes because he liked the Reverend Kerrich so well. We used to have a preacher coming round to conduct the morning and evening service at the chapel so he'd come in to dinner between, it would be our turn to have him about every six weeks. We went to chapel two or three times a day, a service in the morning, the chapel Sunday School in the afternoon and then a service again in the evening. I was organist at the chapel there for thirteen years until 1926.

I went to Littleham school and I left before I was fourteen. I think there was over a hundred there. My sister and I used to wear white embroidery aprons, starched and ironed wonderfully special they'd be and the boys would be running along with these old iron hoops on the roads and if it was a wet day I'd come home with a mud-splattered apron! The teachers were strict, if you were a bit late, I used to live in fear and dread, I used to come in looking at the clock to let them know I was sorry for it! Cos we had to work hard really on the farm, there were so many of us and I used to milk two or three cows before I came away to school. We used to keep about ten or twelve cows. I used to come home for my dinner and before I had my dinner I used to wash the separator, that's what we used to use to separate the milk with to get the cream. Then I used to grease out the tins because Mother used to be very busy Wednesdays baking the bread and cakes in this yer old-fashioned cloam oven. It was on the side of the fireplace, this great place that went back ever so far and you'd have to put in a lot of sticks before it got really hot and then rake it all out. Oh it used to bake lovely, lovely food, lovely bread and cake but a lot of trouble to do. Every Wednesday she used to do it.

We all used to sit around one table to eat, a big farmhouse table. Mother made potato pasties and egg and meat pasties for tea, lads working on the farm got so hungry, there used to be a lot of cooking, the hardest work really. We'd put on a large saucepan for the washing up, that was on the Bodley. You'd let that one out night times and light it up in the mornings, you always had to have lightings about, plenty of sticks to hand.

We used to supply the Rectory with dairy produce and when things were scarce I would be sent down to Orleigh Mills and Mrs Sanders would let us have some cream and butter so we could still keep it going at the Rectory because there were times when we would have it plentiful and times when it would slacken off.

We used to keep pigs and every now and then the farmers used to have one for what they used to call salting in. Mr Jack Cook up in the village that had the long family used to be the butcher. Something to go back on, i'n'it! My sister and I, we used to take it in turns going with Father and Mother to market. They used to go years ago with these yer traps and I think about it often now, when 'tis rough weather and the wife would have to hold up one of these great carriage umbrellas, heavy old things they were, I don't know how they done it really, they must have been strong in the arm! They had big baskets with eggs, butter, cream and hogs' puddings to sell, chickens, 'twas hard work but I got out of that in later years, I think farming got easier after a few years.

Mother used to employ a woman to help with the washing sometimes, like when there was a little toddler around and she needed a little extra help. She'd have someone come in about half a crown a day! I reckon you're glad you weren't born in they days and I reckon I'm glad I wasn't born too early too! All the water had to come from the village pump for those that lived up there, we had our own small pump and it was always air-locked, before you could get any water you had to prime it and then pump very fast to get any water from it. If you left it for a while 'twould run back down and you had to start again. We used to have a big galvanised tub for bathing, I remember my family we used to bath weekends mostly, one after the other topping it up with water from a hot kettle, 'twas quite a job!

At Christmas we hunged up our stocking and we were lucky if there was just an orange and a few sweets, just a few little odd things. They might remember our birthdays if it was something special like a twenty first, otherwise they didn't take much notice. My, when I see the things my grandchildren get provided with now!

Father used to rent the glebe ground from Reverend Kerrich, I think I've heard him say it was sixty odd acres. He used to employ a workman, sometimes we'd have a chap living in the house, that used to be the way years ago. Us children used to help with harvest and there'd be some people around who could come in and help for a few hours, when the weather was right for carrying hay we'd have a few extra helpers come along. 'Twas easier to get people then than 'tis now. After I finished at school in the evenings I used to help with the milking, feed the calves. And of course there used to be a lot of cleaning up to do with so many, one day we used to have what we called bedroom day, clean up the bedrooms, another day we'd do the downstair room. Mondays I used to put all their best clothes in boxes and clean their best boots and shoes. We used to manage somehow, a lot of people today wouldn't survive it!

I married when I was twenty six, the farmers' daughters used to stay at home 'til they got married then, course they don't now and I don't blame them really, I think 'tis nicer if they get out more and know a bit more about the world, they're educated more now. I married Ernest Beer who was one of a long farming family who used to live at Ashridge just about a mile across, we went to live at Hallsannery Farm (a mile from Littleham village.) We went to school together and knew each other there, we didn't keep friends together very long because he had this place to go into so we had quite a hurried marriage really! He had the cage before the bird! He wrote me a letter telling me about the farm he'd been offered, I worried about it really because we hadn't been courting you see, I had to make up my mind so quick because the farm was waiting you see and we were married in a few weeks. But I never regretted it, he was very good and kind to me. We had two sons and two daughters. Years ago they had too many altogether, some of our grandparents had twelve or thirteen!

At Hallsannery we had the dairy with zinc windows to keep out the flies and we made cream. We had the separator, a machine you see which turned around and divided the milk from the cream and the separated cream used to be lovely, well you can't buy it like it now. And we made butter. We had a proper milk scalder, a great big vessel thing, you'd get a fire in under, a furnace and get it really hot and then put the pans down in the boiling water and scald the milk, six pans to once we used to do. You'd put it in the dairy to let it set and the next morning you'd get the skimmer and skim it all off like. Quite a busy job really. In hot weather the cream'd be all thin and you had to put it in the churn for a long time to get the butter to come."

Mrs Beer went to the kitchen to make a pot of tea and as we drank it together I told her about the changes in the village and asked her whether she found life very quiet now after her years of work on the farm.

"Well you can't do nothing about age can you! So long as you can just doddle along from day to day and look after yourself, it's a great thing i'n'it. I should hate to be in a home or anything where I had to be dependant. When you're in your own little home you can just do the little things you feel like doing. The worst of living old is you see your friends and relatives go off, that's the saddest part."

The remorseless domestic toil, long hours spent at chapel, a life governed by tradition rather than choice, Mrs Beer had made me realize that conditions can change beyond recognition within one lifetime. Such a life would be inconceivable to the young couples in the new houses with their fitted kitchens and bathrooms, cars to transport them wherever they might want to go and televisions and music centres to occupy their hours of leisure. But I could not help wondering whether they would look back on their lives with such pleasure and acceptance.

Chapter Six

The Pride of the Housewife

After talking to Mrs Beer, I wanted to find out whether life had been as hard for all women in the village. It is difficult for a generation used to electricity and running water to imagine surviving without them and so easy to forget that it is only recently that such luxuries have transformed village life. I soon found that for many people memories were still vivid on this subject.

Winifred Johns lives in one of a short terrace of small stone-built cottages a mile from the village. I had known her by sight for some years, waving as she and her husband passed me in their Morris Minor when I was out walking and sometimes meeting Mr Johns collecting firewood in the Rectory woods, a tall stooped figure moving slowly between the trees pulling a small wooden cart behind him. I visited her on a raw February afternoon when the woods opposite the little row of cottages were damp and bare and the wet leaves formed a mulch underfoot. Inside the cottage was bright and warm. A fire burned in the grate of the small low-ceilinged sitting room, reflecting in the copper kettles and the old copper boiler which stood on the hearth next to a pair of bellows. A vase of early daffodils stood by the small paned window and an arrangement of red and yellow silk flowers was placed on a table covered with a multi-coloured flowered cloth. Copper plates shone from the walls and the mantlepiece was lined with brass candlesticks and horses.

Winifred Johns is a large comfortable looking woman with a face lined with laughter, she welcomed me warmly and we settled into armchairs by the fire. I asked her if she minded me recording our conversation. "Oh my goodness you'll have a fine old laugh when you hear my voice on that thing!"

"I was born at Clovelly, 1907, and we lived there until 1914 and Mother come to Bucks Cross in the cottage right on top of the road where there's a little lay-by. I got married in 1932 and came here 1934 and here I am still today! My husband lived next door to me at Bucks, oh yes, we used to go to school together, if he was in a mind he'd wait for me to go to school and if he thought better of it he'd go without me!

Gilbert was on the County Council from when he was sixteen I think until he retired. His boss who was in the yard was living in the top house here and this one was empty so he said, why don't you come down live beside of me? We came in and I said, oh gosh, no, can't live yer! You know what 'tis, you go in somewhere where all the paint is chocolate brown and the walls was white-washed, well dirty white-washed, coming up those steps was like coming into an old barn, I said oh us shan't be here very long, and here I am! Fifty five years! By the time we'd gone over it and scraped off all the dirty paint and painted it, and home's what you make it i'n'it. Yes home's what you make it. There was an old black Bodley yer, well we got that all polished up and had that several years.

When we was married, Gilbert's wages was £3 15s a week, you work that out! If he worked an hour overtime it would be one shilling. We managed because we had to. We were asked when we came here, do you want to buy it or rent it, oh rent it we said, we can't afford to buy. I think we could have bought it for about £200, that was a *lot* of money! That was thousands today!

There was no mains water, our well was at the top of the road on the corner. For about three months of the year 'twould be dry! Well then my husband and Mr Cole next door, they dug a well over the road, we rent an orchard over there, 'cos there was a lovely spring up in that covert and they piped it down to the gate. So we managed with that for, you know, so long. We'd fetch it in buckets for drinking water, if I fetched two buckets it might last all day. But for washing Gilbert used to go down to the stream, well they all did, go down to the stream Sunday mornings and fill bungalow baths or ordinary baths for washing the next day. By the time they come home Monday nights 'twould be all empty, they'd have to start all over again! The well was all right when there was plenty of rain and I believe it still does run in there, but it used to soak away and as I say, three months of the year there was no water there. Our toilet was a box affair with a bucket down the bottom of the garden.

I had a boiler on top of the Bodley for the washing but then we got a little bit more acclimatized and we had a Primus stove and I used to put a big boiler on top of that until we had the electric which wasn't many years ago, I should say that must have been about 1952 or 3. The electric was able to pump the water up from the stream, the main river, up into a tank at the top of the house,– the top of the end of the buildings – you'll have a fine old mess there won't 'ee! You haven't got that on? Oh God! So then we could have toilets, that water could pump for our toilets you see so that was a little bit easier for washing and toilets, that was lovely!

Except you couldn't pump it up very well when it was muddy. We didn't have mains water 'til about nine year ago. They came up to Whitehall with it and we signed, oh yes we'd have it, but that was as far as they got, no further, we were left out. When it came that made the world of difference! You can turn the tap on now!

On washday we had trays, big galvanized trays, I had two, one I used to have for washing and the other for rinsing you knaw. Mind you didn't give them quite so much water as you do today! And I must say they used to come out just as clean. I used to boil it up in that one (a gleaming copper boiler on the hearth) then take it out into one bath and wash it through and then a rinse and then another rinse with blue in, believe it or not! Powders then wasn't like they are today you knaw. I never used a mangle 'cos I could wring pretty tight, Mrs Taylor down there would say, well I don't know, you've got strength in your hands, I said well I'm always tearing my pillow cases!

I was cooking on the Bodley, ooh several years, well nearly up to 1950 I reckon and then we moved over to a Primus oven which was very nice but 'twas a bit of a job keeping the pressure up. That Bodley was the pride of the housewife! I'd polish it up with blacklead, well it would come out to meet 'ee at the door. You kept it polished up every day but once a week was when you put a scarf round your head and you got the flue brush and cleaned it and got all the soot down and polished it up again.

Then the electric came, well, electric stove, that was it! Do you know we haven't got any more time now to spare than we had then. I mean 'twas scrub-top tables wasn't it? Lino on the floor, you had to wash that every week or polish it or whatever. Course there was no telephones, no electric. Oil lamps and candles, and if the men went out milking or anything they used to take their oil lanterns. Matter of fact I know one person they said went courting with a lantern, I don't know whether that was true or no! I can't imagine it!

I'd bake bread and make saffron cake, always a pasty on the table for tea, always, which I'm afraid I don't do today. Well he can't eat pastry and if I make it he's got to have more than what's good for him then he suffers. I used to make jam, pickles, well I still make pickles but we're not eating jam like we used to. Cutrounds I still make.

We used to have milk brought to our door in a churn and they'd dip the milk out. That was just after we came here and it was Ashtons up to Thorne, Buckland Brewer. They'd come to the door and we'd take a jug out for a pint of milk.

Sometimes we'd buy a rabbit but Gilbert was no good for shooting, not a bit of good. I never encouraged him to anyhow. I know one day he said, I'm going over to get a rabbit if I can fire the gun, I said well I'll come. He fired the gun, well he didn't hit'n but I saw the rabbit jump and I said come on, let's go home. I said the rabbit's got to be sitting down still if Gilbert's going to hit'n! So he never got his rabbit.

Anyway I reckon that was the good old days, mind you I wouldn't like to go back to all that water-carrying! But they was happy days. Now turn that thing off and I'll make a cup of tea!"

Those who lived in the centre of the village were luckier, there was at least a constant supply of water. One of the wells I noticed in my early days in the village was a hundred yards from my cottage. The pump, for this was indeed the site of the village pump, had been removed and the well itself was hidden by small padlocked doors over which curling tendrils of ivy crept unnoticed from the hedge, softening the straight man-made lines of the doors until they blended into the hedge and seemed a natural phenomenon. It was easy to think that I was discovering something long forgotten. On a misty November evening as the sun went down and leaves lay deep in the deserted lane I could imagine people walking from the cottages with their buckets, meeting and talking as they waited to draw water and returning slowly, their arms braced to bear the weight of the buckets. But I always saw these people in Victorian or Edwardian dress, the women in long skirts and white aprons, the men in smocks perhaps as if they had stepped from a film of a Thomas Hardy novel or a romantic Victorian painting depicting country life. I did not imagine at that time that anyone would remember using the village pump but it is in fact only forty years since mains water came to Littleham. Mrs Badcock who was postmistress for thirty years and still lives in a little cottage in "the Village" was the first to tell me about it.

"We fetched all the water from the pump. And it was brown! The buckets would be as brown as brown. Very irony water but nobody was ever bad with it. It was nice water to drink, very hard, but very cold. If you left it to stand it would have a film on it. It spoilt your clothes so we'd save our own water for washing, as soon as it was raining put something out under the shutes to catch it. We caught all the water we could. Now over where you're to Mrs Beer had the loveliest water, have you still got the well there? One or two used to go there and she'd give them a bucket of water for drinking, she had a pump with a proper little trough. There's nothing like well water. Mr Hearn made a well up in the field for the bullocks and he let us have a pipe and bring it down to the backdoor and that was a help but that was irony too.

The pump was where the new houses are, it was about where the pavement is. Course there was a bit of a do about that because they should have left it, made a feature of it. It used to supply all these houses and it never went dry, he'd go down low but then he'd make again. Some people would open the doors –there were little doors on the front, they were never locked but none of the children ever fell in!– and put the bucket down for quickness, save waiting for it to pump up. Sunday nights it was one after the other, fetching water ready for Monday morning. We used to fetch it in trays (baths) for washing, one each end, but we did catch a lot of water, you'd only use that water for washing when your water butt was empty. You'd save the washing water for the tomatoes. It was only Mrs Beer had a well, all the other houses had to use the pump, the council houses and bungalows as well. East Furlong, they had their own well.

The boys used to fetch the water and they'd kick up, they didn't want to go! Nobody liked water-fetching."

Fetching water was not the only problem. Margaret, who lived next door to me until she and Reg moved into Bideford had other memories.

"There was no sinks nor nothing like that, you'd wash up in a bowl on the table. There was always a furnace in the corner of the kitchen to heat the water. The floors would have been earth of course but I can only remember them being concrete. Each cottage had the toilet up the top of the garden, long old trip! And you'd no toilet rolls, cut up the Radio Times, string it up, that was Saturday morning's job for us kids! But it makes 'ee wonder, you wasn't no worse for it was 'ee. Then there was the job of emptying it, ask Reggie about that! He used to hate that, dig a pit in the garden and make sure not to walk there for a few days! That's why the soil's so good!"

Some of the outhouses which housed the old earth closets are still standing in the gardens at Mount Pleasant. They are small sturdy buildings whose original purpose is clear from the height of the roofs of heavy undulating tiles, not being high enough for gardeners to stand up straight they make awkward tool sheds. In more secluded parts of the village the earth closet did not need to be hidden away at the end of the garden.

"Our toilet was out on top of the garden, well that was quite a walk. And then there was a big improvement, it was brought into the front garden. That was a big improvement, you only had to walk out to the front garden! There was like a form and there was holes cut out in it, a fairly large one for grownups and a smaller one for kiddies and a wooden cover to it. Now without being rude, you aren't recording this I hope! ours used to face the north you see and it was open to the north wind so that you didn't sit there very long when the wind was out to the north! Oh dear, oh dear! I hope you aren't putting that down! It had to be dug out and you'd put it on the garden or if you had a stream it would be fixed over a stream. There it is, time marches on."

As the new houses in the village are sold, vans arrive to install automatic washing machines, tumbler driers and microwave ovens into the fitted kitchens which already contain electric hobs and double ovens. Mrs Badcock remembered how different things used to be.

"We had a furnace for the washing, a big round thing made of bricks with a little grate for the fire and a copper basin for the water. We'd put sticks in to get it hot then boil up the washing. A day's work before you start! 'Twas old-fashioned when you come to think about it. We had a little mangle out in the yard, a rubber one, down at Orleigh Mill they had a great big wooden one and that made the buttons fly!

We had a Bodley for the cooking, kept that going all the time. When we got rid of that we had a range. Course before people had Bodleys they used to cook on the open fire and bake in the bread oven, I remember my sister doing it. She'd light a fire in the oven and get it burning and when it was red hot she'd clear it all out and get the bread in and shut the door up tight. They reckon the bread's beautiful when it's done like that. She'd do the potatoes in there too or a joint if she had one. She had a long chain and hang the kettle on that over the fire.

We had the electric first, before the water. In '47 they were suggesting having the pump brought up, weren't 'em, brought up in the village, another one up here for the people in the village, well that was '47 so there wasn't no water then. It was about '49 I should say. We had the electric before that but I don't know when it was. We had candles, we had an Aladdin lamp, that gave warmth as well as light. When Reverend Kerrich was here we used to have Sunday night services and the church was all lit by candles. We used to go down with Tilley lamps, you could take those out in the wind, people used to manage. Well, let's face it, they used to go skittling, cycling. The village hall was all lit with oil lamps for dances and things. Down the chapel they used to have those big hanging oil lamps, Mrs Parsons, it used to take her half a day to clean them and oil them all up.

You'd go in shopping with thirty bob and you'd go to the butchers and up to the market and get everything, they wouldn't look at it now! A big grocery bill would be just over a pound. Us had more callers, us had bakers two or three times a week, you don't get nothing now do 'ee really. All the callers had horses and carts, the fish man used to come in a little three wheeler, the coal man had a horse and cart, us had more callers then than us do now. The postman used to come with a motorbike and sidecar to start with, then they had vans. Us had more callers than us do now.

Us used to fetch our milk from Mrs Cole down at Middle Langdon. Nearly everyone went to her until they falled out, you never knew how you was going to catch her, she even went for the quietest people. Her falled out with everyone in Littleham but when she was all right you could have her heart. She was a very clean person, beautiful, and she made cream, for 2½d you could have a lovely dish of cream. After that we went to Mrs Nicholls, we'd go down with a can, it was lovely milk. I've been down there many a time on a Sunday morning and waited while she milked the cow."

Gertie Beer remembered her mother making a special drink.

"My father was always very much against drink but we did used to make herb beer for the harvesters, you can't get it now unless you send away for it specially. Mason's herb tonic beer, I know Mother used to make it and it used to be lovely. You put yeast in it and let it stand overnight and then it creams over in the morning, you skim over the yeast and bottle it when 'tis clear and oh, it was a lovely drink. Quite healthy too because it's got herbs in it. 'Twasn't anything to make you feel, well 'twasn't toxic or anything, you wouldn't feel no worse for it, better if anything. Now cider, that's a miserable thing for working on, you feel more like you want to go to sleep!"

Some of the women in the village used to take in washing for others as well as doing their own and most had a period in service in one of the big houses in the area before marriage. No doubt life was far easier for those able to pay for hired help. Vi McDougall lived at Heale House in the thirties and admitted that she had had an easier life than some, but there were still many inconveniences.

"One of the things I remember most is seeing those poor people struggling along with the baths of water from the pump. Even if we had to pump the water into the house, at least we had it there in the house, we didn't have to carry it in. So I think the water and electricity has made a tremendous difference. Have you ever lived with lamps? You see it's such a bore because you turn them up and they blacken and the whole room gets black and the chimney's black. And then if you haven't done them and it gets dark, oh it's all terribly tedious. And the drains of course because you don't have to go up the garden path."

By the thirties things were already starting to change, there were less people employed in domestic service and class differences were beginning to narrow. But there are some who still remember the early years of the century. Did the villagers ever resent those in the big houses and envy their leisured existence?

Chapter Seven

The Big House

There were three big houses in Littleham. It is no longer possible to draw clear distinctions between houses; cottages have been improved, new houses ranging from small bungalows to four bedroomed "executive style" houses have been built, farmhouses have been sold off without land and barns converted. The people who have moved into the village are office workers, teachers, retired solicitors, people who would have lived in the towns earlier this century but now favour a rural view from their windows. Farm workers have to live in Bideford and drive to work every day, having been priced out of their own village. Yet it was not long ago that almost everyone in the village could be classified as either gentry, farmer or cottager.

The big houses, Heale House, The Rectory and Yeo Vale House (actually in the parish of Alwington) provided employment for many people in the village; in addition to the men employed as gardeners or coachmen most young girls had a period in service before marriage and some continued to work part time after marriage. The single girls always lived in at the big house, providing much needed space for younger brothers and sisters in the tiny cottages. There is no doubt that life was hard for the cottagers and it would not be surprising if the contrast between the lot of the employees and the leisured existence of the gentry had been the cause of resentment. However I found that everyone spoke well of their former employers and seemed surprised when I invited them to comment on the injustice of the situation, but then socialism never has found much favour in North Devon. Being, until recently, isolated from the rest of the country the inhabitants of North Devon have tended to be suspicious of strangers but show a fierce loyalty to members of their own community whatever their social standing. I found no evidence of exclusiveness when talking to the older inhabitants of the village though many were uneasy about the more recent comers to the village.

"I think the difference between now and then is people lived in the village longer, they didn't move, they didn't come just to sleep and work, they were village people even in the big houses. Then there was the school, you used to all play together you see, well not from the big houses because there weren't any children there but farmer's sons, farmer's children went to the school."

Gertie Beer, a farmer's daughter herself, remembered the very poor children at the school.

"We all used to play together, we didn't used to look down on anyone nor nothing like that, we all got on pretty well I think. Some of them, such long families used to live in such poverty and poor dears they couldn't keep their families so clean and nice as they ought to have and they used to get what they used to call this yer lice in their 'eads you see. I used to be shy of sitting next to anyone that got it because you know, you could see it sometimes. Oh dear! Then they used to have inspectors coming round and look at the children's heads and if there was anything like that they had to stay home for so long so they all got marked out you see."

The gap between rich and poor was, for many, part of the accepted social order in the early part of the century. There was co-operation between people of all classes and this tended to reduce perceptions of hierarchy. The older people now find themselves on less certain ground.

"I think people were happier then, now there's so much difference between the rich and the poor. I don't know that there's any very poor but a lot's got a job to live I think, if they've only got their pension and they've got to pay their rates and rent too you know. Course there used to be a gentry and people used to look up to 'em and never think no other and they used to work for them and everything used to be happier. Some were very poor, when the pension came in first, they were delighted, they didn't know where – they had five shillings a week, and they thought my, what ever would 'em do with five shillings, they never had such a thing in their life, five shillings for nothing! Course there was the workhouse for people who hadn't got anywhere to go, people used to dread to think that they'd go into the workhouse that they'd do anything to stay home."

Two of Littleham's three big houses are still standing, memorials to an age of social stability when the gentry were rich and the poor could hope for nothing better. Heale House is a large house of mainly Victorian construction which stands between Scratchyface Lane and Yeo Vale Road. The muddy track leading to the house which puzzled me in my early days in the village is merely the back entrance, no doubt the main drive was well maintained although this too is now little more than a track and the house itself seems in need of repair. It has undergone several changes of ownership since being the residence of Captain Bell, one of the biggest employers in the village and still well remembered.

32

"Squire Bell, he was very good and if anyone was ill he would try to help a bit you know. Mrs Bell was very good too I think. 'Tis all a thing of the past i'n'it? There aren't they sort of people about much now or they've gone a different place to live or something. Well there's nobody now in Littleham like that and they were supposed to have plenty of money and they employed so many servants."

Charlie Cook, whose experiences of gardening at Heale are related in the next chapter, found Captain Bell both a fair employer and a source of entertainment.

"Working down at Heale, if Captain Bell was around he'd always come and speak to you, you know. It was 'e that started me off smoking, he used to give me a packet of cigarettes every week! He used to serve all the staff the same you see, he never used to serve one better than the other, all alike. There were four gardeners, two chauffeurs, lady's maid, parlour maid, kitchen maid, scullery maid, cook, there always used to be a heap down there, all Littleham people.

Well now, did I tell you that Mr Bell had us all down there dancing? Oh yes, he showed me the way to dance! I was thankful about it too! Yes he came up to me one day and he said I've been up London or some'ing and learnt ballroom dancing, he said would you like to learn, I said Yes I would. I said I've got no idea about it, rhythm or nothing like that, he said all right. So anyway he got me and there was another young chap just a bit older than me, he had us two in there and he had all the staff indoors in there and there he was showing us all the different dances and there us was gwain all around the billiard table! Us used to go in there, well nearly every night, the trouble was he used to keep us there until nearly two o'clock in the morning! We had a good time though. He'd dance with any of the staff and we'd have a gramophone for music. The time the Charleston come out he learnt that, and all things like that and then there was the waltz of course. I'm glad I did it because I've had a lovely time, I've enjoyed it thoroughly."

Captain Bell was able to take advantage of modern inventions as well as employing servants to make life easier, no water-carrying for the gentry!

"Down Heale House, there's a well at Apps which used to supply Heale House and they paid a shilling a year. So they used to come up every Christmas with their shilling for their water! It was piped and windmills! Those windmills used to pump it to the house. The old man Bell used to come up with the shilling every Christmas, Father used to say it was more a Christmas drink!"

Vi McDougall, whose family bought Heale House from the Bell family in the thirties, found modern conveniences to be somewhat less than convenient. By then things were already beginning to change and less servants were employed.

"The windmills were quite effective for pumping water but of course just when you wanted the wind to blow, it didn't, and people who weren't used to it used to use a lot of water and then we would run out. The windmills pumped the water up into a reservoir and then it came down by gravity. Then the gales would come and the sails would be blown off, my father got very tired of it so when the mains came it all seemed such a joy, now I often wish that we had our own as well but I don't think that *they* like that do they.

When we lived in the big house we used first of all to make our own gas, a very tiresome job. We had a little gasometer and then the stuff, carbide, came in lumps and you put them into trays, there were three trays, and then you filled the other part up above with water then you twiddled different knobs and the water dropped down and turned these lumps into vapour. When it was all finished it made a rather nasty sort of white porridgey stuff which you then had to dispose of. But of course it had no power, it used to give out a nice light but it was very tedious, you can imagine it was a labour. It couldn't do anything but lighting. So then we thought we'd be terribly modern and have an electric light engine which we did but it had very little power, I think it could manage a record player but nothing much else, not even an iron. So when the mains came that was really a joy."

Was Mrs McDougall aware of much social difference between her own family in the big house and the villagers?

"You see in a place like Littleham it was mostly what you might call villagers in the village and then I suppose us as you might say in the big house and there weren't the professional people because mostly the professional people lived in towns. As someone said to me only the other day, well you knew everyone, you could even recognize every footprint! My mother, there was only about twice when she whacked me and once was because Mrs Joy who did the rough, she had just washed the front steps and I wanted to go down you see while they were still wet and my mother said I wasn't to because she didn't want her to have to do them again and so very perversely I was able to creep down the side holding on to the banister so I didn't actually walk on them but she was very annoyed because she thought there was I causing Mrs Joy more work and that was the few times that she gave me a little whacking. So yes I think I was aware. I didn't play with the village children but then I wasn't up there nor they down here."

Captain Bell mixed freely with the villagers and everyone felt they knew him well, consequently he was accepted. Mr Berrold at Yeo Vale House remained somewhat of a mystery and his origin and affairs are still a subject for discussion among those who came into contact with him. Even those who were in his service for many years had no idea what his business was or how he earned his money, knowing only that he was often away on business trips and that his supply of money appeared limitless. He had his own private plane and foreign servants, both of which made him quite extraordinary in the North Devon of the thirties. He might have been quite unpopular had he been less generous with his employees and their families but his Christmas parties are still remembered by many.

"They used to have Christmas parties down there and all the village children used to go and we'd all have a present. He'd hide them all up around everywhere and what you found, 'twas yours. I know I had a little tank, a lovely little tank. After about five minutes, well you'd have four or five things you'd found, oh 'twas a lovely party! Mrs Cook worked there so she used to ask and then we could go you see."

Yeo Vale House, although only a mile and a half from Littleham was in the parish of Alwington. It was demolished in 1973 thirty five years after being abandoned by its owner. Mr Berrold proved as strange in his manner of leaving his home as he had in his stay there. After a dispute with the neighbouring farmer over a tree which had been cut down, he announced his intention of leaving the house forever and, so the story goes, flew off in his aeroplane and was never heard of again.

"Yeo Vale? 'Tis gone now. He left there you see, Mr Berrold, he only went because there was a tree there and he worshipped that tree and he went on holiday and the tree was cut down, coo he was mad. And he never lived there again, he said it's for the birds, the house is for the birds now. He was supposed to be working for the Germans so some said, he was always a mystery. When he went he treated all his staff to his cottages, those that lived in them, but he would never come back again."

Others suspect more sinister motives for his rapid departure.

"They suspected him of being a German spy, when the War broke out he cleared off, he had a plane and flew off."

The house stood empty for many years, gradually falling into disrepair until it became a danger to the children who played on the once elegant staircase and a nuisance to the farmer who lived in the converted stables adjoining the big house. Advertisements in national newspapers failed to attract the attention of the Berrold family who appeared to have disappeared from the face of the earth, so Yeo Vale House, inhabited since the fourteenth century, was demolished. If any of Stephen Berrold's descendants should return to claim their inheritance, they will find that the once grand gates open now only on an empty field, the merest undulations showing where the house once stood.

Littleham's third big house was the Rectory. The Reverend Kerrich was incumbent from 1909 until 1933. and is still remembered for his kindness and generosity. He was "one of the real Littleham people" and was loved by church and chapel-goers alike. Gertie Beer told me her memories of him.

"Reverend Kerrich was such a nice man, I remember he conducted my father's funeral and he said everything that was kind and nice. When *he* died my mother went and she said she felt awful sad because there was no one there to speak so nicely as what he deserved. He used to give a Christmas tree and a treat for the school children every year, a present for each child. And you see people were poor, living in a poor old style then and it was all so appreciated, the children really appreciated it then. More went to church then, more than go today especially when Reverend Kerrich was there. He had three or four services on a Sunday and he'd have a good congregation. He *was* good and he'd go and visit all round".

Others had amusing memories of him, it does not do for a Rector to be too holy.

"The Reverend Kerrich was a very popular man, yes. Sir Hugh Stucley used to own this property and he used to have all the shooting and they used to rear a lot of pheasants and let go. I can see the Reverend Kerrich down here in one of our fields, they'd have a special stance for everybody, and I can see him shooting, I can picture him now. Who's going to listen to all this? I ought to be careful what I say! Well I can see the Reverend Kerrich, bang, bang and miss the pheasant, bang, bang and miss the pheasant, unload his gun and throw the empty cartridges down and stamp on them! I don't know if you were near enough if you'd hear him swear or no!"

The Rectory stands in a sheltered south-facing position on the edge of the village, its Georgian windows looking out over gently sloping landscaped gardens planted with camellias and rhododendrons to fields and wooded hills beyond. It can be reached either through the village or by way of a stony drive which winds up through woodland from the Bradworthy road. This drive is now a favourite route for walkers and horse riders but storms in recent years have sent rivers of water gushing over its previously nurtured surface, making it impassable to cars. In this more realistic age, money is no longer available for such labour-intensive work.

"Reverend Kerrich had a horse and carriage and the old horse used to do all the work in the grounds, pick up the leaves and that. You wouldn't see a weed in that drive or a leaf out of place, perfect, far better than Hobby Drive."

"He had four gardeners, that's what they houses was for, Red Cottages and Old Moor, rectory houses, staff houses, they've got the coat of arms of the church on them. I don't know that they all lived there because Bill Brend, he lived in your old house. The Rector used to visit people and bring round the magazine. He had money of course and he only had the one parish. More like a gentleman Rector."

It may be that Littleham was lucky in its gentry, certainly things did not always run so smoothly in neighbouring villages.

"In Monkleigh years ago you had to toff yer 'at to the vicar and people in the big houses. I know Father give me hiding once. This gentleman came up with 'ees horse and I was just walking along and he looked at me and said, "Oi! Open the bloody gate". So I said "You get off and open the bugger yerself" and walked on. Two nights after Father had to go up there with a parcel and he told Father what had happened and Father come oom give me a hiding. So I said, if he'd have said please I'd have done it and Father said well, what did he say. So I told him exactly what he said and Father said right, I'll go in and tell 'ee. And he went down and he took me down with'n and he said now then Colonel, or Major was it, you didn't say what you told him, you told the boy to open the bliddy gate. Oh yes he said, I did. Well he said, manners maketh a man, not 'ees money. Next time if you say please, he'll open the gate, if he don't, you tell me."

It is often the newcomers to the village who are blamed for the changes which have taken place but change is inevitable when the younger generation is exposed to different ideas, whether they are newcomers or descendents of old village families. One former farm employee I spoke to was painfully aware of the difference between generations.

"I told him once, it was hard when I gave up working down there for him because I was part of it. As a little child I mean, you collected the eggs then from – there was one hen laid in the piggery and one in the loft, then you'd go back in and sit up beside of her on the form by the big long wooden kitchen table you know and clean the eggs with a bit of rag, not like you clean them today! And I said you know, I said I've been associated with the family, I said your grandmother and your mother and now you but I said I'm afraid with the next generation it's full stop. And if they begged me to work for them I wouldn't, they're just different, a different type altogether you know and I've got a feeling that the next generation, his family would look down on me, I really do, so I wouldn't work for them."

It is unlikely that England will ever see the reappearance of a social class as favoured as the gentry were until mid-century. There may be more wealthy people in Britain today but few are accorded the respect experienced by earlier generations, nor perhaps is it desirable that they should be, such respect being founded on the acceptance of a social order which condemned many to a life of unremitting poverty. Those living in poverty today are only too aware of the injustice of their situation although it could be argued, judging by the people I spoke to, that ignorance can sometimes mean bliss.

Chapter Eight

Charlie Cook

After my immediate neighbours, Charlie Cook was one of the first people I got to know in the village. It was his son who was to be seen repairing tractors and villagers' cars in the little yard next to one of the council houses near my cottage and it was Charlie who would call out a friendly greeting as he worked in his immaculate garden. He was already retired but still did some part-time gardening in the village. I would see him returning for lunch, a small man in a cap pushing his bike up the hill, a big bunch of dahlias or a few vegetables for his wife balanced on the handlebars and always he would smile and wave. Charlie's wife died a few years ago and is missed by many in Littleham. He and his son now live alone but Charlie still has a smile for everyone.

Charlie is one of the old order. He has stayed in the village all his life and has never wished to live anywhere else, only moving house once and then only fifty yards down the road. He was one of a very large family living in a tiny two-bedroomed cottage, the endmost in Mount Pleasant or the Village as Charlie would say. His father followed an age old pattern of working which is seldom seen these days, not working for one single employer but rather finding work where he could and using a variety of skills. When Charlie himself started work at Heale House it was more by accident than design but he chose to remain a gardener all his life. His story is best told in his own words.

"I was about three months old when I came to Littleham, that would have been, well 1905 I was born. I was born at Landcross, right beside the church. Well there was four of us born down there and the other five born up here, nine of us. The funny thing about it was, there was nine down at the farmhouse too, eighteen children in two houses. I remember the times when there used to be over a hundred up at this school up yer. My father was a gamekeeper, he was all sorts, he was a labourer, he slaughtered pigs, he used to do practically anything, he was very clever. It was like he'd say, he could make a rick or he could thatch a rick, he could do anything on the farm he could and he'd work for anyone you see. So that's how it went, he had to get out, he had about half a crown for killing a pig. If a man reared a pig and got it fat for himself, Father used to go and kill it and the next day go and cut it up for him and they put it in the old trendle, what they used to call a trendle, and they'd salt it and have meat for a twelve month near enough. Father was also a rabbit trapper so he used to very often bring home a rabbit for us to eat. There was one thing about it, we never starved and what ever was put in front of us, we had to eat it, no use saying I don't like that, if you didn't eat that you could go without! We didn't have a lot of meat but we had soup, vegetable trade, fried potatoes, things like that.

Mother had to work pretty hard, she had to go all up Littleham Court doing washing Mondays, only for about a shilling a time, 'twas awful. Then of course she had to bring all the water up from the old pump yer, do you remember the pump? We used to have to carry all the water for washing from there, course we never had no water laid on then. Father was pretty good, he used to see to all the firewood and things like that you know. He used to till his garden up there, we always had plenty of vegetables to eat. He used to keep two pigs at a time, one he'd salt for us then he'd sell the rest of it you see to pay for the food that the pigs ate. Mother used to bake her own bread and I can remember her using the bread oven, an old thing with a handle sort of, right up beside the Bodley. I had sisters so they had jobs to do and when Father got older I used to do the garden for him until I left. On Tuesdays Mother would walk into Bideford to do the shopping in the market, push the youngest of us in the pram, walk home again with the shopping.

We'd have our roast on a Sunday, that was general practice back then I think, if you didn't have a roast dinner you didn't have anything! I had to go to Sunday School, you all had to go to Sunday School, that was in the schoolroom up at the Chapel. But I finished up, when I started work I went to church then. We had a little pair of knickers sort of, cordyroy trousers, we used to have to wear they though daily so didn't have much different Sundays. I think I used to wear what you call a sailor suit too. Then of course you used to have nail boots, oh those nail boots, we never had no different for Sundays. We used to come home and say, Dad, I've got a nail out of my boot, and he used to have to put another one in! Thick old leather boots they was.

Regatta! We always used to have a day off for Bideford Regatta! It was just the one day then, we had an old aunt over at East-the-Water and we used to go over there to have our food. That was our day out that was. We might have another day at Westward Ho! My mother would drive a horse and a long tail-cart with a bit of straw and have all us children up there in the cart! Or we'd go to Instow, there'd always be a lot of people on the beach there, they used to call it Babyland one time!

I had me mates and we used to play football, hopscotch, things like that. We used to play a game called Crowners, it was one side trying to get the other side and you'd catch hold of the one that was in your way and chuck 'em down! It was a rough game, a very rough game! They were all pretty good the boys and girls here, there weren't any we were told not to play with, nothing like that, they seemed to be all one family here. I don't know anybody here now.

We was always a bit afraid of Father, if we'd done anything wrong we'd be punished for it, have a hiding, have a thrashing! It was only harmless fun we'd done, not like they do now, not stabbing people nor nothing like that but we used to be a bit artful sometimes! We used to hang up our stockings at Christmas but the next morning there was nothing in them. We might get an orange but that was all, so many children you see, they couldn't do it. We'd have a Christmas dinner, pheasant or some'ing like that. I can't remember I had anything for my birthdays.

There weren't much room with nine children and only two bedrooms! We slept all in around together, there wasn't a room for the boys and a room for the girls, nothing like that. I was the only one that stopped there til I was married except my younger brother, I hadn't got no cause to go out lodging anywhere because I was working round yer you see.

I started gardening when I was fourteen year old, I was down at Heale House, that's where I started. I was there ten and a half years. A man came up and said to my father, "I hear your son's leaving school, us could do with a boy down here, clearing up." My father said "He'll come right on Monday morning", he never asked me nothing about it, I must just get out and go! I was well trained, I started from the beginning and I worked me way up, before I left I got charge of the greenhouses for the last two years so I was well away with that. I did have a chance to learn the chauffeuring down there but I thought to meself, well I've learnt all the vegetable things and all that there but the thing I haven't learnt is the greenhouses so I said no, I said I'll finish me gardening job now. It was Captain Bell there then, he was a very good bloke, he was. I worked from quarter to eight to six, we'd have a break for a cup of tea then I'd walk home for my dinner, used to take me quarter of an hour to get home, quarter of an hour to have my dinner and quarter of an hour to get back! So I had quarter of an hour easy, not doing nothing. I was paid fifteen shillings a week to start, I gave it all to Mother! There weren't no pocket money nor nothing like that then.

All the staff used to go to the County Show, it was held at South Molton one year, they had a bus to take us there. I made friends at work, 'specially the girls! We'd go out for walks or to dances, I was very fond of dances, oh I used to love it. There was very often dances up here and we used to go to Monkleigh, Buckland, Abbotsham, used to be lovely at Abbotsham, used to enjoy that! All around. We often used to go to dances after I was married too, we'd walk all over the place. They was the good old days, they really was, no mistake about it. They used to have very good bands back in they days, tisn't like all this old business now! It was proper dancing then, waltzing, things like that, foxtrots, now there's just all this old banging, knocking your 'aid about!

We used to dance down at Heale as well and in the end Enid came down there too 'cause her father worked down there you see. And the funny thing about that was, I used to bring 'er 'ome when she was gwain to school! It's so funny i'n'it how it turned out. She didn't used to go every night, only just when she could lie abed next morning, on Friday night or some'ing. But it was very funny, never got any idea that I'd ever marry her then! And the thing was, I've been miles courtin', I used to walk to Eastleigh sometimes. But you see that's how I was, I was always very friendly with the girls, I could get on better with girls than I could with men I think! Yep! 'Twas lovely, 'twas very nice. 'Tis all over now. I've had a lovely life, no mistake about it, I'm not grumbling, there it is, everything comes to an end dunnit.

From Heale I went to Yeo Vale House, Mr Berrold who lived there had an aeroplane of his own, he took me up in his aeroplane! He used to take the staff up, all of the staff, he went up twice with us, so there we was whizzing round up on the top! Then he left the place and so I left and went on to Portledge, from Portledge I went to Westward Ho!, that was during the war time then and I had to grow vegetables for the Army sort of, there was Army camp right next door. And from there I went to my last place up Old Barnstaple Road and I was there thirty three years, that's where I finished up. I got round on my bike, always.

I remember starting on fifteen shillings a week, then I think it, well I can't tell exactly but I think it went up to about two pounds, something like that, less eighteen pence for an insurance stamp! The next rise was four pounds and in me last job I went and asked for four fifty, oh yes that would be all right. I came home to Enid and I said I've got fifty pence more a week! So of course when I finished in there it was fourteen, fifteen pounds a week, 'twasn't no big wages. But the wages have rose tremendous since I stopped work, they wouldn't do it today for what I was working for!

I left that house in 1932, I got married then and came right down here (50 yards away) so I haven't been no further than that! The funny thing about it was, I bought this piece of ground out here before ever I knew I was ever coming in this house to live. Before I was married I had the chance to buy that piece of ground so I did, on spec. Well I kept pigs and poultry out there for a time. One day I was down here, outside there, tending to my poultry and the lady who lived here came out and she said "Oh, are you thinking about getting married?" Well I said I haven't thought about it, not exactly, I said I *shall* marry the girl I'm going with but I haven't made no arrangements. Well her said "We're leaving here, shall I put in a word for the council for you?" so I said yes, that would be a good idea. So anyway she went in to see the council, yes that would be all right, so I started paying rent soon as ever she left in September and in the January I got married! Enid lived up here at Red Cottage, just the other side of me, I used to go miles courting and finished up right home on me doorstep! I've had a good time and I've travelled 'tis true. When I used to work into Bideford with the lady in there, I worked there for thirty three years, she was very good to me and Enid so she used to send us off on trips, she sent us to Ireland, Scotland, Isle of Man, she was a very good lady. So I've had a very nice life, I'm getting old now but still, don't matter!"

Chapter Nine

A Pattern of Work

Charlie Cook started his working life in the village at Heale House, moving to Yeo Vale House when Heale was sold and then finding work outside the village when Mr Berrold mysteriously disappeared. It is difficult to establish how many people worked in the village during the early years of the century, Charlie was the only one in his own large family who remained at home.

"I don't think there was a lot worked in here, they always used to go off to Bideford and places to work. But of course there was more farm labourers around then than there was today, there's hardly any farm labourers around now. Every farm around here had one feller anyway and there were more farms then. In my family all the girls went out of the village, they used to live out you see. So it come that it was only me left really, but then Mother had the last, a last appeal! she was forty eight when she had the last child. (The ninth). So of course he stopped home until he got married because he worked at Bartletts and he used to go to and fro to Bideford. But before that I was the only one left home, the others had all gone out."

Other people see things differently.

"Most people worked in the village, gardeners or farmworkers. the Rectory had a lot of gardeners and so did Heale House."

The last available statistics can be found in the census of 1881. Places of work are not of course listed but study of the types of occupation suggests that most were working within the village. Out of a total population of 363, which was made up of 191 females and 172 males, the occupations were as follows:

Farmers: 10.
Farm servants (living in): 14.
Farm labourers: 9.
Butcher/farmer: 1.
General labourers: 26.
Excavator: 1.

Carters: 3.

Mason: 1.

Wheelwright: 1.

Blacksmiths: 2. (The house now known as the Old Forge was not a blacksmiths shop in 1881, the two listed worked at Langdon Cottages and Summerhill, the latter rejoicing in the name of Arscott Crocker.)

Millers; 1 + son. (at Edge Mill)

Carpenters: 6.

Boot and shoe maker: 1.

Glovers: 4.

Innkeeper: 1.

Grocers: 3.

Dressmakers: 5.

Laundress: 1.

General servant/domestic (living in): 5.

Cooks: 2.

Housemaids: 2.

Kitchenmaid: 1.

Coachmen: 2.

Footmen: 3.

Gardeners: 4.

Nursemaids: 2.

Brewery cellarmen: 1.

Accountant: 1.

Schoolmistress: 1.

Naval pensioner: 1.

The glovers would have worked in Bideford's glove factories and perhaps the dressmakers used to work in the town, other than them it seems likely that the majority worked in and around the village. There is a surprisingly small number of female domestic servants, and only one brewery worker in spite of the fact that Apps Brewery was then in its heyday. Perhaps the numerous "general labourers" worked wherever they were required, including the brewery. It seems unlikely that labour was brought in from Bideford, two people in their late eighties could remember their parents telling them that the cottages in Mount Pleasant used to be the homes of the brewery workers in the last century.

Villages were largely self-sufficient in labour because of the pattern of land ownership: landowners needed labour, those without land lacked material resources and therefore needed work, it was a simple reciprocal arrangement. The only workers likely to leave the village were domestic servants, especially females, who commonly lived in and often went to other villages in North Devon to work. Less and less people have found work in the village over the years, inevitable of course when so much farmwork is now mechanised and servants no longer employed. Teenagers are now very unlikely to find work in the village, but this is a relatively new development, certainly many of their parents still had the opportunity to do so. Until Margaret moved into Bideford a few years ago, she had always worked in the village.

"I worked down at Heale Farm for twenty three years. I went in the glove factory in Bideford when I left school but I couldn't stick being shut indoors so then I went over there and I stayed! I did all sorts, inside and out.

We all used to go potato picking, we used to take the children and the prams, pack up the bottles and nappies and flannels! 'Twas a bit of fun, we was all there together and it was nonsense all the time. 'Twas hard work, we'd be a bit stiff the first couple of days but after that it would wear off. When the children were tired they'd curl up on a bag on the ground and have a sleep."

The potato pickers can still be seen working up in the fields in the autumn, their bent backs and sack aprons as unchanged as the rich brown earth below their feet, only the tractor creeping up and down the rows indicates that this is the twentieth century. There are less of them now than there used to be but they all still come from the village or, having moved into Bideford, return for the potato harvest. There are no young faces amongst them now, who knows who will replace them in a few more years? The inclination for this type of casual work is dying out yet until recently village economy was dependent on it. Charlie Cook's father, a man of many skills, was typical of his time and the habit of turning one's hand to whatever work needed doing continued well into this century. Charlie again:

"I used to do a bit of harvesting for the farmers before I left school, well most did then. The thing about it was in they days if you was harvesting, they always used to bring out tea at five o'clock to you in the field, us used to call it drinking, drinking time you knaw. And another thing, if you were down there threshing on the farm, you'd always have to go in and have your midday meal with them. The men would very often come down to help in the nights after work, it was all a bit extra money."

Winifred Johns also used to help on local farms.

"Ooh harvest, out in the fields, yes used to do that, helping with the hay harvest. Well the men did when they came in from a day's work, they used to work from seven to five, have their supper and when Mr Taylor was here doing hay up in the field they'd be there 'til ten o'clock. Gratis! I mean you didn't expect to be paid. You ask anyone to do the hours today! We didn't expect it! I know one time Gilbert had some cigarettes given him and you'd have a supper and we were quite happy, quite happy to do it. You never expected to put your hand out for money, never! Do it for the pleasure, we used to enjoy it, there'd be a bit of a crowd out there and 'twould be a bit of fun really. You'd get a supper p'raps about ten o'clock but I've never known Gilbert take any money for harvesting.

I used to help down at Mrs Taylor's here when they'd killed a pig, to make hog's puddings. Mr Cook used to go around killing pigs, so he used to come down and kill the pig and clean it up, hang it up, then they used to cut up the pig you knaw and she'd sell bits she didn't want then she'd salt in what she wanted and then set sail and clean the innards for the hog's pudding. Water, water, water, water, you knaw until that was all done and then she'd make the hog's pudding. Hog's pudding day was a lovely day to go down there, a nice greasy day 'twas! And they were bootiful I must say 'cos I knew where they'd come from you knaw."

Winifred's mother had her own special role.

"Mothers used to have their babies at home and there was always somebody to help out. When Mother was at Bucks Cross, people there would always book Mother like they would book a midwife, baby's due next month, whenever, and I would like you to come over and look after the house, cook for the children that was there, cook for the husband. One woman said, you can't do better than have Mrs Prouse because she said, if there's nothing in the cupboard, her'll find something to cook up! Make a potato pasty with lots of cream or a squab pie or something like that."

There were also more idiosyncratic ways of earning money in the village. Lionel Badcock remembered his childhood exploits.

"Another thing I used to do which was rather wicked really was to catch moles, I used to catch a lot of moles. Skin 'em. John, 'e used to catch about eight or ten a day, I didn't catch as many as that. We used to nail all the skins on the door, when us had got about forty or fifty send them away to Horace Friend in Norfolk, 'e'd send us back a cheque for about four pound, 'e'd make them into coats, moleskin coats. He used to supply us with all the labels, stamps. He'd put them in grades as it was, certain times of year they weren't worth very much. I used to go all in around the Rectory, catch them in traps, I had about twelve traps, put them in the runs. In they days us used to see 'em, mole hills. Farmers used to like us to do it. Us always used to discuss it up school, how many us had caught!"

Today's teenagers are more likely to earn money babysitting than catching moles and harvesting is almost totally mechanised, gone are the days when half the village would turn out to help. But farming requires a chapter to itself.

Chapter Ten

Farming

Farming has changed more this century than ever before. This change from labour-intensive to mechanised work has had a drastic effect on village life as the farmers used to be the biggest employers in villages. Farms used to be smaller and more numerous, in 1881 Littleham boasted ten farms including Gregory's Langdon and Middle Langdon, now private houses, but then farms of 35 and 22 acres respectively. As can be seen from the census, each farm employed several men and no doubt many more would help out during harvest. The use of horses provided more work, where several horses were kept a horseman was needed to care for them and the blacksmith was kept busy. It is hard to imagine now a countryside without the drone of a tractor engine, always somewhere, ploughing, drilling, spraying. The heavy horse belongs to another era when work was slow and steady and the farm worker was not distanced from the earth by metal and noise. It is too easy however to be sentimental about farming with horses, the work was hard and heavy and it is likely that when Wordsworth watched "him who walked in glory and in joy, Following his plough, along the mountain side," he was too far away to hear the curses as the ploughman wrestled with the plough and stumbled over the heavy soil.

The mechanisation of farming has taken place so quickly and so thoroughly it is easy for the younger generation to imagine it has always been so but even those in their forties and fifties remember horses being used. Alan Marshall still pursues the old self-employed pattern of working despite being one of the younger generation. He is a familiar sight around the village with his mop of greying hair, usually seen through the windscreen of a car or van, lorry, Landrover or even vintage car, for Alan collects anything with four wheels. He will do plumbing or electrical work, is an expert on Rayburns, moves and delivers anything which can be moved or delivered and knows the car registration number of everyone who has ever lived in the village.

"Us kids, when we were going to Littleham school, used to ride on the tractors and trailors to get down to the fields down around the parish hall to help carry the hay. I remember Edward Stevens cutting it with horses, he had a massive horse called Prince and this Prince used to follow the cows when they were going from School House Farm out to the fields, he used to trot along with them. I remember once being very frightened because for some reason Prince had been left behind and he guessed where the cows were and came full gallop round those bends by Apps. And he was a massive carthorse and there he was coming towards me with these massive hooves.

Anyway us kids used to help with the turning and loading, we used to mess about a bit with the hay, we were really there for the fun of it. We used to sit up on top of the trailor, it was a bit bumpy. It just shows how things have developed, on one occasion Edward Stevens was cutting corn and he had a Fordson tractor which he'd bought new and this thing always used to be playing up, stopping and messing about. He got fed up with it and he took it out and he put the horses back in the binder and went on cutting with the horses.

Then in '51 (another farmer) had a new Ferguson tractor, ODV 51, and of course this was like a modern car compared with the old Fordson which went along about 3mph. This one had lights on it and you could slip along in top gear, you could do nearly 20mph! We thought we were well away if we got on that one!"

Fred, who preferred me not to use his surname, has seen farming change completely within his lifetime.

"Mr Stevens was the first one to have a binder in the village, three horses pulled that and the sheaf used to come out the side. Wonderful age really because there was the reaper, the binder then the combine. Then to begin with they used to have a bagger, the corn used to go into bags. It was the same with hay. My father used to say, they'll go to school on a rocket dreckly!

I used to milk a couple of cows before I went to school, take the cows up the other end of the farm. And same in the evening, fetch the cows when I left school and milk two or three cows, help generally. Seven year old you'd be milking a cow sitting on the girl's knee, trying to get a drop of milk. When you were nine year old you'd take a horse and a cart to Bideford and pick up half a ton of coal, you wouldn't load it but when you were ten year old you were expected to unload and carry the coal where it had to go. I mean you enjoyed it, just like today they look forward to driving a tractor, I couldn't get up behind a pair of horses quick enough. If they said, oh you can go up with the plough, well you did, you felt proud to be able to do it."

In the first half of the century it was still possible to start farming in a small way and slowly expand, buying up more land when the money was available. Small farms are very rarely available today and farms to rent even harder to come by, making things very difficult for the farmer who is not already well-established. Mechanization may have made farming less physically exacting but it has not provided more leisure time; there is always pressure to produce more and machinery needs constant upkeep.

It was from William that I learnt most about the old ways of farming. William is in his ninetieth year, one of a family that has been in farming for many generations, he still lives on the family farm and likes to do what work he can despite his age; one afternoon when I went to see him he had spent the morning clearing the ditch which runs along the narrow winding lane leading to the farm. He is one of a generation of farmers who had to struggle for all they achieved. After death duties were increased in 1909 many estate farms were sold off and the tenant farmers had to find ways of scraping together enough money to buy their farms if they were to have any chance of progressing; some of those who were unable to find the money were forced to leave. Obtaining loans was not the straightforward matter it is today and borrowing money was seen as little more than criminal by many.

Like most older people who have lived in North Devon all their lives he was very wary about meeting an "outsider" and insisted he had nothing of interest to tell me. However when he learnt that my grandfather was Mr Friendship, a baker and restaurant owner who until the end of the Second World War catered for farmers on their visits to Bideford Market, he welcomed me as "one of us" and after a little initial nervousness at the presence of the tape recorder, talked freely and needed few questions to prompt him. He is a charming old man, tall, upright, the only sign of his age being in some loss of hearing which sometimes led him to answer quite different questions from those I had asked but we spent several very enjoyable afternoons together. He has his own sitting room in the family farm, a room which must have remained unchanged for many years, furnished with an old Aga, a couple of comfortable armchairs, a large dining table and a dresser. He has old books and photographs to remind him of the past and a telephone with amplification to keep him in touch with his few remaining contemporaries. He asked me not to use his surname in print and to leave out any details which might identify him "because I've never been one for advertising myself about".

"I was born in the parish of Wembworthy, I was three years old when Mother and Father came down here. My grandfather lived down here you see, he moved down here from Lower Boundstone. I can just remember the house at Wembworthy, I was only three years old but I can just remember one thing, there was a little stone wall out around, not a very wide front garden, and my elder brother and me, he was three year older than me, we were always told to be careful not to fall out over that wall. I took my mother back there again when she was eighty to see where she started and I could see that wall! Now then I ain't helping you anything about Littleham! I remember my grandparents on both sides, my mother's side were connected with Littleham, they go back to 1842 in the churchyard, they were at Lower Boundstone.

I was born in 1900, I go with the years. I'm a Victorian really! If I'm spared till next February I shall be ninety. I remember my mother saying that the great thing in life is to take everything in moderation and I've lived to think how true the words were. I had one brother and two sisters, they're over eighty now. I lost my wife and brother in the same year. There've been a good many troubles and trials in life. When I was young they told me, my generation, if you don't save any money all you'll get when you're seventy is ten shillings a week and that's all my mother and father got. So it meant that we had to keep our nose to the grindingstone and you see you keep your nose to the grindingstone so long, you can't take'n away! You can't alter that's the worst of it, you get in a rut and you can't alter.

My people used to go to Bideford, Wesleyan Methodists in Bridge Street. The Sunday School was ten o'clock in the morning, the service was eleven o'clock and the Sunday School was again half past two in the afternoon. You had to clean up your shoes, boots, we never wore shoes, clean up your boots you wore weekdays and we would walk into Bideford from here for ten o'clock, go to the Sunday School, our mother would drive in with the pony and jingle for the service, we'd drive home, have your midday meal, walk in again by half past two and walk home again afterwards! You don't know what you've got to be thankful for! You hear about the good old days, now what do you think about that!

Life was very hard on the farms, it was remarkable how they lived. As I look back I think our parents were wonderful people, I don't know if my grandchildren will think that about me! What was so different about the old people, they knew where they were going. They hadn't got any money, they could work as long as they liked but there was no money to be had. Everything they had to live off came off the farm, they'd till their own garden and they'd kill their own pig, never had roast beef, if you had a piece of beef it was real luxury, you couldn't afford to buy anything you see. It was remarkable. I don't know how they reared us really but I suppose everything was in comparison. To live on the farms you had to work like a horse and live like a pig! You know they talk about the good old days but they that talk about it don't really know very much about it! There was no let up at all. Well the same applies now with my grandchildren, if you've got livestock you see you've got to work seven days a week, there's no question about that, you can't neglect it at all. But there it is, life goes on. With all the troubles and trials I've had, I can still feel I've got a lot to be thankful for 'cause I've had the two best things a man can have and that's good health and a good wife and I've been blessed in that way.

My wife was one of thirteen, seven girls and six boys. Where did I meet her? Well I don't know. In the old days there used to be Christmas parties you see and you'd meet when you were thirteen, fourteen year old you see, you'd be invited all around to parties. There used to be sheep- shearing parties. You couldn't get any labour and the farmers would club together and you would have a sheep-shearing day and then I would have a sheep-shearing day. Well I would go and help shear yours and if I had any workmen or sons I would take them and we would shear all day. And in the evening if we finished up fairly early, we'd have a dance in the barn you see. So what happened was, you'd get your sheep shorn for nothing and I'd get mine shorn for nothing. But you hadn't earned very much when you'd done it because even when I started farming and had sheep, wool got so cheap as sixpence a pound and I said I wasn't going to sell it for that so I kept it for four years until it was worth a shilling. We'd have an old gramophone at the party, a phonograph with a cylinder. You would know everyone for miles around really.

I don't remember having any drink at the sheep-shearing parties, maybe at the Christmas parties they'd have some. Well of course they used to make their own wine, they used to make their elderberry wine and their rhubarb wine and sloe gin and all this you see, that would be perhaps more intoxicating than the wine is today, we weren't allowed to have it! At harvest time they'd have in a cask of cider, cider was the farming drink. Men would work all day just for a quart of cider! I can remember seeing my father with a firkin of cider, he'd push his stick up through the handle and go away to the field. There used to be an old chap in Littleham called Harry Nichols, he was rather a clever chap at dealing with sick animals, he used to live down Langdon way, this is going back a hundred years or more, I've heard my parents talk about it, I'd almost think the house must be gone. He'd got a field or two and there was another chap used to come and help him cut a bit of hay and he would have a cask of cider. He said well we might as well have a drink before we start, so they sat down had a drink, sat down had another drink, sat down all day drinking a cask of cider, had to come back next day to cut the hay! That was my mother's story, that's not mine!

I left school when I was fourteen and came to work on the farm. When my brother was fourteen my father took him to Smithfield Show in London but when I came fourteen the First World war was on and I couldn't go so I never went to Smithfield Show until I was gone fifty!

There was no money in our day but there was more fun, you would meet up, but even my grandchildren, they haven't got time to have a day off hardly. There's more money about, there seems to be loads of money around for everything. I suppose they do have fun now, I don't know, but it seems to me there was more time to enjoy yourself. Everything's got to such a pitch today that it's all very finely balanced, mind I'm only outside looking in over the fence but it seems to me that people have got a lot of money but they've got a terrible lot of expense, there's very little in it when they've finished even in the farming industry today. It wouldn't take very much to bankrupt a lot I wouldn't think. People have run away with such a lot of buy now and pay at Christmas, my generation can't understand that. It was almost like going in front of the judge to go and see your bank manager but now they come outside the counter, help yourself! That's the difference.

There seemed to be more help about and you see, harvest time, if somebody was working and they were walking down the back road here, if they saw you were harvesting they'd come in and give a hand. But that's all gone and done away with you see. And then perhaps all they'd do was stay to supper, there was always this big supper for anyone who'd helped on the farm you see. And I can see my mother in there dishing up the supper for them but they'd do this out of the kindness of their hearts you see, that sort of feeling's all gone now, there's no casual labour about at all. And not only that, the machinery's got so good and so expensive that it isn't no ordinary body's job to do it, not just working with the old fork and this kind of thing. All the tools now have got a seat with it so you sit down and do it!

I can remember having the yoke to carry the pails, I've worked one of those just once, it took the weight, it was surprising how easy it made it. When they had to do it all with handwork, they found ways of easing the situation. When the first riding plough came to the parish, it came to Littleham Court and it was a two wheeled plough with a seat on it you see, the man drove it and sat on the seat instead of walking along behind. It was a marvellous step forward although our family never had one of those. When this riding plough came in, a man came in who was passing down the road and he came in the field where the plough was working and he said to the farmer, this is a new plough I understand, made to kill the horse and ease the man!

You don't want any Devonshire language I suppose, I'm rather lax in that, I use it quite often! 'T I neevur, if you asked me a question I might say, 't I neevur, that means, what I know for or as far as I know. Dregstool, do you know what that is? a threshold! I think it's best forgotten now, the younger generations, they don't use it, they don't know anything about it.

The postman, he was a remarkable man, he was called Short, you've heard of him I expect. He used to walk from Bideford Post Office to Buckland Brewer and deliver the post, come back through and deliver in Littleham and come down our back road, he wouldn't come into the farm but there was a box in at the gate and you'd fetch your letters. He'd be there, he wouldn't vary five minutes, it was remarkable when you come to think about it.

We had two teams of horses, there was the head team, the head horseman, he used to treat his horses like, well the fatter he could get his horses the better he liked it. There was always a horseman on the farm, permanant. He used to keep a hutch in the corner of the stable where he kept the corn for the horses and that was like the holy of holies, you weren't allowed to look in there, he'd lock that hutch you see and he'd come every week and the farmer would give him so much corn and that would have to last his horses for the week you see. We boys, we would work the odd horse you see, sometimes there was two teams and sometimes there was an odd horse. The horseman who was here in my boyhood used to walk out from Bideford and he'd be out here six o'clock in the morning and tend to his horses then in the winter he'd be ploughing all day. They used to like horses with a lot of hair round the fetlock and at the end of the day the fetlock would be all dobbed up with mud. They weren't allowed to take the horse into the stable until they'd been with the horse to the pond and got all this mud off. As time got on, whether the farmer got wiser or lazier I don't know but he bred the horse without any hair!

After the First World War my father got a horse from the Army, it was all horses that did the work in the war you see, and this horse had been wounded in the shoulder and after we had it, it swelled up and mattered out and the veterinary took out a piece of shrapnel. But what I was going to say you see, this horse, we used to call him Gunner, he couldn't start off at a walking pace, he had to go away at a gallop because that was the way he'd been trained. We used to put him in beside our horse to go to plough, work as a team, Gunner would be galloping and our horse couldn't keep up to it! My brother was called up to go in the war and I should have had to went, I came eighteen when the war ended you see.

In my young days my father used to grow an acre of potatoes and he used to allow people to come out from town and till three rows of potatoes. They had to find the seed and he would do the work and they had to dig. It was in return for this that they had to come and help in harvest time, there was no money passed, that's how you lived you see, that's how they got their work done. There would be about seven or eight of them would till about three drills of potatoes, if you had a great long field then two drills would do.

I can remember my father taking me to Torrington market and buying a cow and a calf and in those days you'd put the calf up in the cart and the cow would walk behind. They had a trap, a market cart where they used to put the big hamper in the back, well that's where the calf would be. I had to walk behind the cow! That was the good old days, you'll be glad you weren't born then!

My parents always kept a few pigs. Charlie Cook's father, he was the slaughterman and he used to come and kill the pigs. We had to boil up water in the furnace, a big copper furnace that used to be out in the wash-house. He'd say, well I'll be down half past six, well that meant we had to be out about five o'clock to get this furnace boiling, if 'twasn't ready when he came, if he had to wait too long, he was so booked up he would go away and leave yours you see. Oh yes it was quite a business. He would have a rope that he would put in the pig's mouth and you would have to stand and hold the pig, hold the head up as high as you can and he would stick it in the throat. I used to hate the job really but I've held a good many pigs for him. If you didn't hold'n exactly steady, if he didn't catch'n first time, he would let off to you! You had to held'n until all the blood was run out from'n see, well then you have'n down on the floor and have this boiling water and scrape'n. He'd got like a funnel he used to scrape with and he'd scrape'n. There was a little hook on the end and he'd pull off the hoof, pig's trotters they used to call them. And then you'd hung'n up and he'd open'n down. He was a clever man, Charlie's father, he was a chap of several trades, he fitted in with the gentry as well as the ordinary people.

There used to be a slaughterhouse at Apps. Coming home from school we'd go in around, I went to school with Fred's father you see and he'd say come in around. So we used to go in around and be looking in the slaughterhouse door where Grandfather Withecombe was slaughtering. Whether we got a nuisance or what but when he thought we'd been there long enough he'd pick up a bit of fat and fling, we'd skedaddle then, we knew it was time to go you see! And another thing we used to do, Apps used to be a brewery in my mother's time and there used to be, they used to make what us used to call pop and there used to be special bottles with a glass marble. Well anyway all these glassy marbles was kept in under the vault, at this end of the house there was a little hole that us used to crawl in under and come out with a handful of glassy marbles if you was lucky you see! We did this so many times before Freddy's grandfather saw us at this yer business, there was one time and no more!

My father used to go to the Sheep Fair at Barnstaple, we'd go with him to go to the pleasure fair but by the time he'd finished with the sheep, he'd be ready to go home. We never stayed long at the pleasure fair! All the cattle went by road, there used to be special drovers who earned their living at it, they were independent and you'd hire them. They had wonderfully well-trained dogs, it was marvellous what those dogs would do. There was a drover coming down the road with I don't know how many cattle, one of them jumped in over with another man's cattle and he could stand in the road and send in his dog and pick out his own, that don't happen very often. The drovers used to come from Parkham, Holsworthy, Bradworthy, Stibb Cross, Torrington of course, they would do all those and take the cattle as far as they needed to be taken. From Bideford market, all the cattle would go down Bridge Street and over the bridge, everybody stand back! You can't imagine it now!

My father bought the farm, it belonged to the Stucley estate. I understood death duties hit the estate hard and to pay the death duties they had to sell some of the land. It was very difficult, it was a struggle to find the money. Looking back it doesn't seem much money compared to the prices they pay today, however anyone lives today with the price it's making I don't know I'm sure. It's always been a struggle in agriculture, even today the farmer is working two days longer than the average person and getting less pay for it. When you get a bit extra money, there's plenty more things brought along for you to spend it on. If you want to make a lot of money you must say no to everything every year! When I was in business, I daresay this was more than fifty year ago, I said to the wife I'm going to make a New Year's resolution, I'll say no to anybody who comes selling anything this year. I said no to everybody, even if it was to my advantage I said no, I wouldn't have it! They couldn't understand it, the regulars!

It was never a very big farm, I believe years ago it used to be three hundred acres. Well then it got dwindled back in my father's time to about a hundred and thirty or something like that. It got sold away and parted up, this was a hundred and fifty or more years ago I expect. You see the farms went smaller, well now they're going bigger, it's funny over the years. It was easy enough, the young farmer could get in but 'e's got a job to get in today, yes. And if there's any more than one to a family 'e's got a difficult job, because the prices, it's the same with houses an' all, it's all gone ridiculous 'a'n'it. But in my lifetime it's never been wrong to buy land, I could have had the best land in the parish if I'd had the money. You see people would come around and ask you to take their land, you can't imagine it, people didn't want it. A lot of houses had two or three acres tacked on to it and they'd ask you to take it, now everybody's starving for a bit of land if they can get hold of it. There it is."

"The thing about getting old," William told me, "is you know nothing's going to change. If I'm spared till next year I know I'll be doing exactly the same as this year, except you won't be coming to see me anymore." I hope William will be "spared" to see his words in print, and I will still visit him because his obvious delight in recalling the past is such a pleasure to hear.

Chapter Eleven

The Farmer's Wife; Annie Palmer

Gertie had told me a certain amount about her life after she was married and others had been at pains to point out that things were not easy for farmers' wives, who had farmwork to do as well as their domestic work.

"The farmers' wives, they had their work cut out, they used to help with the milking, the pigs and the calves, the poultry, if it was hay harvesting they'd be out helping with that. Some of them used to sit in the market and of course all that's gone, they don't sit in the market anymore."

The importance of the role of the farmer's wife is illustrated by Gertie's hurried marriage; when her future husband was offered the opportunity of a farm the acquisition of a wife was a matter for some urgency, she was needed to manage the dairy and feed the calves and the poultry, all clearly defined tasks for the farmer's wife who needed to be skilled in such matters; a farmer's daughter who was already used to the work was an obvious choice. It might seem that there was little room for romance in such a decision but there are many worse reasons for marrying, a marriage between two individuals of very similar social backgrounds who work together in complementary roles stands a good chance of success.

The opportunity of renting a farm was not to be disregarded. The difficulty in obtaining land had led many people to emigrate in the nineteenth century, a large proportion of them farmers' sons. For some marriage came first and the farm later, one of these was Annie Palmer. Of all the old people I visited, it is Annie I think of most often. I had barely known of her existence as she had been confined to her home by arthritis for some years but when people learnt what I was doing, they all told me I must go and see her and, without exception, spoke of her with great respect and admiration. I asked a mutual friend to approach her and when she said she would be happy to talk to me, arranged a time to visit. Her home, Rudhabridge Farm, is a mile from Littleham on the narrow lane that runs between high hedgebanks to Monkleigh. It is situated on a corner just above the River Yeo and as I got out of my car I could hear the murmur of the river alongside the usual farmyard sounds. It is a farm that can have changed little over the years. Bantams peck at the verges around the entrance, a black and white sheepdog with a penchant for chasing passing cars lies watchfully at the roadside, a cow lows from one of the barns above the farmhouse. There are no smart milking parlours to be seen here, no shiny new farm implements, but there is an air of tranquillity, a sense of peace which has been found through tradition and hard work.

I walked across an area of short rough grass to the farmhouse, a long, low, whitewashed building typical of the Devon longhouse; unlike most houses which have now been converted entirely to living accommodation this one still houses a barn under the same roof. I knocked on the low door, then remembering that Annie would not be able to leave her chair I went in, calling out a greeting. I found myself in a narrow passageway with a door to each side and hearing an answering call, opened the door on the right. Annie sat very upright on the edge of her armchair next to the fire, her small bright eyes shining like buttons. She greeted me eagerly and at once started to tell me about her childhood as I struggled to find my bearings and set up my cassette recorder. As I settled down to listen I looked around me. The room was square with a low ceiling, dark paintwork and brown patterned wallpaper. Next to Annie's armchair was a trolley of dark wood on which stood a cup and saucer and the telephone, her contact with the outside world. There was a long farmhouse table strewn with newspapers, a large rolltop desk, photographs of her grandchildren and great grandchildren on the tiled mantlepiece. A door led to the stairs, another to the kitchen which was a big rather bare room containing a large table piled with groceries and an old Rayburn which smoked quietly in a corner, blackening the wall above it. The house seemed rather neglected, lacking a woman's touch perhaps as Annie could leave her chair only with difficulty and her son was kept busy on the farm which he worked singlehanded.

Annie's chair faced a single small window which looked out on to a concrete block wall. Here she sat listening to her radio which was always tuned to Radio Devon, the day broken only by lunch which her son John came in to prepare. He came in once through a rear door as we talked, waved and threw some more coal into the smoking Rayburn. The monotony and loneliness would have depressed most people, but not Annie. She talked animatedly not only of herself but of the phone-in programmes she heard on the radio, chuckling at the foibles of the people who rang in; her grasp of current affairs was impressive. As she talked to me of the past, the hands twisted by arthritis lying inert in her lap, she gazed out at the blank wall through the mist of failing sight as at a screen upon which her life was being played, and her face shone with pleasure.

Annie did not have an easy life. She did not make much of the hardships and it was not until I listened to the tape afterwards that I realized from the dates she had given me that her husband had died after only a few years of marriage, leaving her with three young children to bring up and a farm to run. This she did with a minimum of help even managing to buy the farm after a few years, a remarkable achievement for a woman at that time. She spoke clearly, each word carefully enunciated with only an occasional hint of a Devonshire accent.

"What year I was born? April 21st 1896, in Alwington, in the cottage, there was an old cottage where Kingsley Cottage is now. I was born in the old cottage then it got rather old you see and my father built Kingsley Cottage in about 1900.

I went to school in Alwington, it's the village hall now. We had to walk to school and there was no wellingtons in those days neither but we managed! We had lace-up boots and capes instead of mackintoshes and umbrellas. We had a Miss Partridge at school and she taught us reading, writing and arithmetic and we had drill with dumb-bells and we had singing lessons and she taught us sewing and knitting, really all that we wanted to, well to make a living of I think. We didn't have science nor French nor nothing like that like they have today, well we didn't need that, no one had it then. The boys did drawing while we were doing needlework. We used to sit out in the yard knitting when it was fine, some had long families and they used to always bring a second lot of stockings in case anyone hadn't got any knitting, we'd help each other out like that you see! Course they used to knit all their stockings years ago, right up to their knees, we used to. All black ones! Wool was only about sixpence for a two ounce pack. Course we didn't have any hot dinners nor nothing like that so Mother had to pack up pasties and sandwiches and cakes you know, bread and butter. There was just fires each side the room, well it was a long room, if it was very very cold I think the headmistress used to give us cocoa but there wasn't no water, not much water there, 'twas rusty so we had to take lemonade and things like that. 'Tis much better today! They get their dinners, don't they, if they like to. I left when I was fourteen. I'm the only one left in my class, they'm all gone.

When I was fourteen I went to live with an uncle at Fairy Cross Post Office, me grandmother was living then, I used to help her then she left and my sister came on then, used to be the cook, housekeeper. 'Twas rather, well, we didn't know anything different you know. There was the post work to do and we kept a couple of cows and had to milk them, scald the milk and make cream, we sold cream and milk. People used to

buy the skimmed milk, they didn't have new milk in those days, t
had the milk after the cream had been taken off. Well they say that's
best really, that's what they seem to be aiming at now, have the m
with no fats in it. A lot of people bought it but then it was only about
penny a pint then you see, people in the village used to come and have
pennorth every day. Then we had some fruit trees and used to sell a few
pears and things like that. Course my uncle was a blacksmith as well, he
was the farrier as well as the sub-postmaster, my father worked with him
as well, in the post office or in the blacksmiths shop. There used to be a
Mr Mason lived at Portledge and he had big pheasant shoots, they used
to post perhaps twenty or thirty brace of pheasants, only just tie them
round the neck with a label, they wouldn't go far like that today!
Someone would have them!

I used to cycle a lot, we cycled to Bude one day, four girls. We started
at quarter past five in the morning and we had breakfast at Kilkhampton
and we got on to Bude in the morning and cycled home again at night
and got home again about ten, that was during the war, well, the First
World War. The roads were very muddy, you had to get off and lift your
bike out of a rut. People going up the road, the older people used to
take their skirts up at the back and trip along like that! 'Course they
done the roads then and it was better though the parish roads are rather
wet now aren't they? They don't keep up the parish roads, not like the
County roads, I suppose they haven't got the money so then they can't
do the work, can 'em? I don't know what it'll be like when we get this
extra rate, this poll tax. I remember when the cars came in first, Dr
Toye had one first then Mrs Hamlyn at Clovelly Court, they used to
make a lot of dust!

Then I married a farmer, we waited six years to get somewhere to live
because he wanted, my husband wanted a farm you see and they were
rather scarce then to be let. We came here sixty one years ago, yes. My
husband died in 1937. He was wounded in the First World War and he
was all right for five or six years and then T.B. set in you see, he was ill
for four years. We had three children.

To start with we didn't sell our milk to the factory, we used to make
butter three times a week, we had a separator you know to separate the
milk from the cream, scald the cream and then make the butter and take
it to Bideford Market. We used to grow potatoes and vegetables to sell
as well and we'd take rabbits sometimes. There were dealers opposite
the market who used to take rabbits too. I sat in the market until I was
seventy six! 'Twas nice going to market, I used to like it, I went every
Saturday. My husband used to take me in in the horse and trap and I'd
sit in the market until about twelve o'clock then do the shopping and
he'd fetch me back again. 'Twas all right in they days, we'd see a lot of

people and it was a nice day out but the worst of it was you'd got to come home to work! I remember your great aunts, the Miss Friendships! They were there opposite the market. They used to carve great joints of meat and people used to go in for a quarter of meat you see and some cutrounds and that would be their dinner. Lovely meat it used to be! Well of course it was big joints in those days. 'Tis different in the market now they say, it used to be all farmers or small-holders in there with their produce.

We kept a few sheep, now we've got more sheep than cows! We've got twenty cows and the milk goes straight to the dairies now you see, every day, that makes much less work indoors than there used to be. In the summer it was rather hard making the butter because you've got to have it cool else it won't, well it wouldn't come, as they say, we had to get up fairly early in the summer. I suppose work never hurts one, it hasn't hurt me, not much any rate! I know one person who was a hundred and two and she was a farmer's widow and she said the reason she lived so long was the hard work and the country air!

We kept two horses to work on the farm then and we had all the implements for horses. Course now we've got three tractors so we've got implements to suit the tractors, 'tis much quicker! We used to employ a man when 'twas a bit busy. Hay harvest was hot work then, you had to turn out and make it and pitch it to a cart and then pitch it on the rick but now of course you turn by machinery, 'tis much quicker today, much better! The neighbours would help, my husband had a cousin farming just above here and he would send a man if we were very busy. 'Tis rather hard work, 'twas, doing everything by hand.

I used to feed the calves and the fowls and I used to help milk, that's how it is I've got bad knees they say, with sitting down, we used to sit down on a stool and milk by hand. Now of course machines do the lot. We didn't keep as many cows then, we used to keep about eight. 'Twas rather, well, hard work 'twas, I think farming was hard work but then everybody that was on a farm was doing the same work. Course you get your easier times as well as your hard times, when it was a wet day it was easier. 'Tis easier working today than it used to be, riding a tractor is better than walking after horses! I used to bake everything but bread, we had a baker call twice a week. As you get older you've got to buy more, I can't stand to do anything much now, all I do now is answer the phone! I used to hire a woman to wash, she used to come Wednesdays. That was after the children came, I couldn't do everything, I had two boys. Then there was the gardening to do too you see, we had to keep the garden going. I'm afraid 'e 's rather rough now because John, well he's a farmer, he isn't a gardener, they say a farmer never makes a good gardener and gardeners never make good farmers!

We hadn't got any taps in they days, we used to bring it in in buckets. We always washed with soft water, everybody did, that came from the rain you see. We'd wash in trays on a form, we'd light the furnace every Monday morning or Wednesdays when Mrs Parsons used to come, we'd boil up the clothes. Course there was no spin dryers in those days, it was rather a job drying the washing in winter time but we did have mangles. We used to put it up in the field to dry, we're under the wind down here. We'd bath the children in front of the kitchen fire in baths, galvanised baths, carry kettles for the water. Our well was up in the field then we brought it down to a tap at the back door, outside the back door, but now we've got it let in to the kitchen you see, and taps upstairs as well.

I went to the Methodist Church every Sunday, I'm a Methodist you see and I went there all the time before my knees is bad and I can't get into a car now so I've got to stay home. Yes, I've always been there. I got to know some people in the village, Mrs Stevens who used to be the school teacher, the Headteacher, then there was Miss Olive Kingdom the primary school teacher, a Mrs Rosie Brend used to keep the shop up there, down near the pub, there wasn't any public house when I came there. Then there used to be the smithy, Mr George Copp, all the farms had horses then you see. Mr Sidney Brend was the butcher, he didn't have a shop, he used to go round the country with meat.

In the evenings there was sewing and knitting to do, I used to knit socks and things like that. My husband gave me a sewing machine as a wedding present! I never went out, not like they do today. I didn't ever go to a dance but I have been to a whist drive. There's bingo these days of course. The only time I've been around is when the Women's Institute had an outing and we used to go to Exeter or Plymouth or Newquay, Bristol's the furthest I've been I think. Of course we used to go to Buck's Mills sometimes before the children came and Portledge we've been to a good bit when I was at Fairy Cross and we've been to Clovelly two or three times. I've never had a week's holiday, only when I went to hospital when I was seventy-six. Well John's never had a holiday, only when he went to have his appendix out. Course you can't leave a farm, specially with the milking.

John does the shopping Saturdays, I phone in the order for the grocer, Mrs Beer in Honestone Street, and John picks it up. I miss going out but you get used to it you know, I see a few people come in and Jean tells me all the Littleham news. I go to the Torridge Hospital Tuesdays and Thursdays, they fetch me with an ambulance, we go around Torrington and Parkham and pick up the elderly people that can't walk. I like going, we have quite a nice time! We have coffee and biscuits and then there's lunch about twelve, then in the afternoon we have a social hour, games or quizzes, I like quizzes best!

There's one person who goes there who's got bad hands and she can't do anything, it's rather miserable I think, I'm thankful I've got two hands, I shouldn't be able to manage at all if I hadn't I think. I can get in and out of bed all right so I must be thankful for that, hands is most important. There's someone else who can't remember things, I wouldn't like that. I can't see to read now, I used to like to read but then there's some who can't see or hear.

You didn't hear so much about stealing and murders years ago, I think 'tis getting worse and worse now. Years ago they'd only shoot birds and rabbits, there was nothing like that in our day, no. I used to know everybody in the parish and everybody seemed to be honest, there was nothing like that in those days, it was a peaceful time. I never heard of anyone getting a divorce! I suppose they had to put up with it! Make the best of it! Course now a lot of the women's got careers and they can go back to it if they don't like housework, I suppose that's the cause of it. It's sad to see all my friends gone. Still some live on and some go quickly, I don't know why I'm sure, different breed I suppose!"

A year after I first visited her Annie died in hospital after a brief illness. Did she, I wondered, see her final stay in hospital as a holiday? I like to think she did. I went to her funeral at Littleham Methodist Chapel where she had worshipped for many years. The little chapel was full, there were many familiar faces but others I did not recognize, mostly middle-aged or older faces with strong placid features typical of those of the Devon farmer. Faces which, like Annie's, have thrived on a lifetime of fresh air and hard work.

Children at Littleham School, 1905

Gracie, Jack and Gertie Stevens outside Boundstone Farmhouse, 1907

Village Fete at Littleham Rectory, 1915

Advertisement for Apps Brewery

A ERATED WATERS.
———:o:———

SODA, SELTZER, LITHIA,

POTASS.

LEMONADE, GINGERADE,

EFFERVESCING LIME JUICE,

MANUFACTURED BY THE

WEST OF ENGLAND AND NORTH DEVON MINERAL WATERS CO.,

FROM THE

CELEBRATED APPS SPRINGS.

E. PHILBRICK, Proprietor.

___

APPS BREWERY ALES,

From 1/- to 1/8 per Gall.

These Ales were analysed during the trying summer of 1876, and pronounced Pure and Wholesome.

ADDRESS—

E. PHILBRICK,

APPS BREWERY, BIDEFORD.

Horace Beer winning the high jump at Littleham fete, 1954

Littleham fete, 1954. Alan Marshall on the right

Glennie at Crossways, 1989

Gertie Beer

Winifred and Gilbert Johns

Maud Badcock

Charlie Cook

Annie Palmer

Chapter Twelve

Journeys and Diversions

Annie's only holiday in ninety three years was a visit to hospital. It is true that holidays are a comparatively recent invention, only becoming popular with the advent of rail travel, but one might have expected at least some of the older people in the village to take up this new invention with enthusiasm. The only exception among the people I talked to was Charlie Cook who was sent on holiday by his employer; Winifred Johns was quite clear about the popularity of holidays.

"Nobody expected a holiday you know! When we had our last holiday it was 1956! You didn't look for holidays. You didn't hear of farmers going away, they went to market and that was their day out, how could they just close down and go off? And as for going abroad, well that was foreign, they wouldn't do that."

There were days however when work could be forgotten for a few hours. There has been a fete organised either by the Church or the village itself for as long as anyone can remember and it has always been one of the most important days of the year for the village. Charlie Cook's earliest memories of fete day go back to about 1910 and he has looked forward to the occasion every year since then:

"Have you heard about the Church teas? Well we always used to have the harvest festival tea down on the Rectory lawn, that was a lovely day, I used to enjoy that! You used to meet all the people, well all the parishioners I think used to come. We used to have the tea out on the lawn, well the weather seemed to be better back in they days somehow, I don't know, I may be wrong. Then they'd have a wooden skittle alley take down there, play skittles and there was sideshows and everybody was happy, it was a really lovely day. I've seen photos only the other day of all those old people, well they was old then because I was young, well they all wore these yer old-fashioned hats and all that there on.

There's been a fete ever since I can remember, I used to show up there with vegetables, there used to be a vegetable show, they used to have a big marquee see and I used to show vegetables and Enid used to show flowers. Us used to be down here fete day, five o'clock in the morning getting things ready to take up there! Yeah, I won quite a lot of prizes, I was delighted with showing stuff. Everything seemed to be going with a swim."

Some things never change it seems. The day of the fete is still a day when everyone in the village can come together and work for a common cause, though there always have been differences in opinion and complaints of certain people not pulling their weight, and doubtless always will be. It remains to be seen whether the new generation of villagers will be prepared to work as hard as those in the past: certainly the village is unlikely to see any as devoted to the cause as Margaret whose cooking has become legendary, the fete has never been quite the same since she and Reg left.

"I always made two hundred pasties for the fete and loads of cakes and what have you, oh yes I gave it all. I'd do the cakes and sponges Thursday and the pasties Friday, I've been up 'til two o'clock in the morning cooking before now because you had to go up to the hall in the evening to get things ready then come back and cook again. Everyone pulled their weight and done their bit then."

Now that opportunities for leisure are so numerous and varied, it is inevitable that the importance of the fete should wane a little; nevertheless it is a tradition that is far from dying out and has changed very little over the years, Annie Palmer could have been talking of the present day when she remembered the fete in the thirties.

"I used to help with the bran tub at the fete, get a lot of packets for the children, they'd be threepence or sixpence. Then we used to have a garden show as well years ago and there was cookery and different things you know. Cyril Lyle used to do a good deal for that, he was a gardener. There'd be lots of different stalls as there is today, and races for the children and a gymkhana. It was a special day for everyone in the parish."

Other diversions have now disappeared.

"The Hunt Ball,– that was the highlight of the year, nearly everyone in the village would go, it was an excuse to get dressed up. It was proper dancing, not that jigging about like 'tis today. The church used to have a dance, and the W.I. I believe but then the bands got so expensive and people were living so near town that they could go into town to dances and they gradually dwindled away. The skittle alley used to be laid up with tables from one end to the other full of food, there was pasties, trifles, everything you could think of. Whoever was organising the dance, whether it was the Hunt, the W.I. or whatever, they would do all the food."

"When there used to be dances up there, my gar that used to be wonderful! Dance! What we used to call our evening off, all us on the committee for the fetes and that, we'd be working all the blimming time up there and then in the night, it was our night, we used to go up there and dance and do what you like!"

The fete and the dances were the high spots of the year but there was time for other amusements during the year and no doubt they were needed as a welcome relief from the endless toil and remorseless domestic work. Winifred Johns told me her memories.

"We used to have picnics, take the children down in the field all the neighbours together, they'd love to go in the river of course. We'd say, now if you want a picnic you've got to gather the sticks from down there so that we can make a fire. So of course that kept them quiet for a bit.

Living down yer, I didn't see people much until I joined the Institute. There was one before, about 1940's I should think but how long it went on I don't know, it didn't last all that long. Well then about the 50's they started another one that I went to, well then we knew everybody you see. We were about thirty I think, well then they start dwindling off or going away somewhere. But yes, I enjoyed that. We got down to about fourteen, fifteen and of course it was the same committee doing it all all the time and nobody changed over, I believe I was secretary about seventeen years. So then we stopped, the one going now is the third you see. I thought, oh, I can't give up Institute so I started going to Abbotsham but I never belonged there. So friendly they were, I never belonged, it was so funny, I don't know.

We used to have a lot of whist drives, a lot, ever such a lot of whist drives and the Christmas one was the big one where we'd get turkeys or geese or chickens for prizes and we'd get over forty tables and we'd have them in the hall and the skittle alley. But that gradually dwindled out. It's a bingo craze now and I can't stand that! I went a few times and 'twasn't that I didn't win cos the first time I went I won a nice piece of lamb, they said, oh, beginner's luck! I said, well it might be but I don't know that I like it that much. I went a few times and I won in the draw and then I won a few sausages, I said oh get off, I don't like that! I'm half way through, I want to come home! I'm fed up I said, looking at this old thing all the time. I said to Gilbert one day, I'm going up to bingo, I said I'm stuck here every night, I'm going out for a bit of social life. Well you sit there and it's eyes down and eyes down, then it's goodnight everybody and you'm 'ome! Oh no, I don't like that! I can't stick that!

We used to have our own amusements. Evenings, the top neighbour, Fred used to come down and Gilbert and him used to play bagatelle. When the Rawles went there it was darts was the craze, they would come down and play darts or we would go up there. But that thing (television) spoilt everything! We were the first to have it round here and three or four of them would come, they wanted to see the football, cup final or something. Oh yes, come on, I'd say, we'd 'ave a cup of tea, oh 'twas lovely! Well next year they all had their own televisions and of course it all went. Now I wish'n further!"

One is unlikely to meet anyone during an evening walk through the village today. The lanes are empty but for an occasional passing car, the doors of the houses are shut and the glow of the television screen can be seen from each window. The advent of the car and the television have probably changed village life more than anything else, everyone I spoke to had something to say about life before and after television.

"Mrs Hearn was the first to have a television in Littleham, she had it for the Coronation I think, then Mr Withecombe and us had the third. Mother used to go town and I'd have 'em all in yer, full up to watch the cup final, that went on several years. Then there were the concerts used to come and entertain in the villages, Ducks and Drakes they called themselves, Dr Ruddock was one of 'em."

"I think television has killed amateurism because people expect costumes to be good and not still showing safety pins and that sort of things. Though I understand the youth club concerts have been well supported."

"In the olden days there was the lady in the cottage that I can mind, and Mrs Clements and my mother and they would visit one another and have a game of cards, they would have a game of whist or something or other. I mean they hadn't got television so they would have a game of cards. Mother would sometimes make rhubarb wine, that was good, lovely, they all used to make their rhubarb wine and go and visit one another."

Rhubarb wine was, no doubt, innocent enough but there was an older tradition of heavier drinking. Hoop Inn in Littleham closed in the thirties and childhood memories concern the outward appearance of the building rather than the goings-on within, but no doubt it was well used. The presence of Apps Brewery in the village must have done much to encourage the habit of regular beer-drinking, it is said that the brewery workers were allowed a daily ration of a gallon of beer. It seems that for some, this habit continued well into this century.

"I think we used to drink more in they days you know, whether it was because of the brewery or what I don't know. Mrs Westcott, she liked a drink. They were stone people, quarry people, she'd come home a good many times and fall asleep at the bottom of the drive."

It was inevitable that leisure pursuits should be centred in the community as opportunities for leaving the village were limited. Apart from shopping trips to Bideford and visits to relatives in neighbouring villages, many people never left Littleham, so there was one annual event which was awaited with much anticipation. Annie Palmer and Gwen Barrow:

"I used to go on the Sunday School outings with the children when they were small. We used to go to Woolacombe, Ilfracombe, Bude, Plymouth. We'd hire a bus - or perhaps two buses if there was several people going you know - and take a picnic. We went to Cornwall several times."

"The furthest we went was on the Sunday School outing, if we went to South Devon it was something really grand. We'd have one of these charabancs, different from the modern day coaches. There was usually someone sick on the way! If it was a wet day the windows would get all steamed up and if you opened a window somebody would complain! We all used to take a packed lunch, the mothers used to be pretty busy getting up early packing up a terrific lot of stuff, they would come too to look after the children. I remember going to Paignton one year and that was wonderful, there was a footbridge where we could go and look down out over to watch the trains, it was terrific."

Such diversions could only be very occasional and provided great excitement for village children because they were so different from the day to day pleasures. But a change from familiar surroundings is always welcome and every opportunity of leaving the village, even if only for a few hours, was taken in spite of the fact that transport was rarely available. It would be inconceivable to most people living in Littleham now to walk the three miles to Bideford, especially as walking in North Devon inevitably means walking up and down steep hills, yet the walk was undertaken lightly until comparatively recently. It is only in the last fifteen or twenty years that it has become commonplace for each household to own one, two or even three cars. Mrs Badcock remembered outings from the village with pleasure.

"In the early days us used to go walking, always on a Sunday and you'd see other people and they'd join with 'ee. Sometimes we'd walk to Gran's up to East the Water, us have walked there many a time, walk!

People used to walk to Bideford, we always did on a Saturday, or there was a bus from Orleigh Mill, us have walked down there several times, it was 10d to go in, now look at it! There was Mr Hills and Western National. There were taxis, five shillings a journey, Mr Ellis the taxi man, brought us 'ome heaps of times, five shilling. There was always someone else going to town to walk with as a rule, up the hill, Upcott Hill, I suppose us was younger and us used to take it all. Mrs Clarke, Rector's wife, her used to have a pony and jingle and her'd pick up anybody on the road. We'd walk down the hill to Upcott, lovely i'n'it, used to be, years ago, but 'twas steep coming back up with the pram and the shopping.

There was no schedule like there is now, if you didn't git 'oom 'til seven o'clock of a Saturday night well then you didn't did 'ee, tidn't like you had to be home to see the television. In the market 'twould still be busy, three o'clock in the afternoon."

Margaret told me that things were still the same in the sixties.

"Us had to walk into Bideford to do the shopping, you could get the basics in the village but you still had to go into town to get a lot of things. Us used to walk in Fridays and get most things but if us wanted anything extra us had to go in again Saturday! Us used to walk in the top road by Jennetts then go back by Upcott with the pram, kids, shopping! But you didn't think nothing of it, used to look forward to it. Once you had a car it made you lazy. There used to be a taxi service, Mr Ellis used to come out Tuesdays and meet at the Crossways, anybody wanted to go would meet down there and share the cost of the taxi, it was hard luck if you were the only one but mostly there'd be five or six. If you'd got kids you couldn't go."

Winifred Johns was more fortunate in her mode of transport.

"We used to cycle to Bideford to do our shopping, oh yes, cycle down town and brought home our shopping, a basket on the front or a box on the carrier, Tuesdays and Saturdays, market days. Why we've got to have so much in the supermarket today I'll never know! I was only saying to Gilbert, breakfast time I think it was, well you know I'm just thinking how we used to enjoy going into Bideford in the morning and it was an effort to come away you knaw, you'd see people and there was nice shops to look in and go around,- ten minutes is long enough in town for me now! Every Saturday, when we couldn't get the petrol, we used to cycle out to Bucks Cross to my parents, and every Sunday, that was our weekend."

Charlie Cook's first experience of cycling was rather frustrating.

"I always remember when I had my first bicycle it was too high for me! Instead of going right around with the pedal like that, I used to go half way and back like that! We cycled to Landkey and back like that one time, me brother was courting over there, there they was cycling away beautiful and I was coming along behind, over and back, over and back but I got there in the end! A gang of us chaps used to very often ride our bikes all down round Clovelly on a Sunday afternoon, we used to go miles on those bicycles. Most people had bikes in those days, they were very cheap then."

He also had memories of outings to Bideford, though not for shopping.

"We'd go into Bideford every weekend, Saturdays and Sundays. We used to go the pictures or the pub Saturday nights, that was our own night when we'd do what we liked, girls didn't go in the pubs you see. Sunday night it used to be walking up and down the Pill, everybody used to be down there, chaps and maidens. You'd go on and you'd stop and talk to some and then no, I'll go on with somebody else, you'd go on with somebody else and then you'd say "What about going for a walk?" That's how it all happened you see, then you'd arrange to meet her the next week or something like that."

Vi McDougall at Heale House did not have to walk to Bideford but journeys were still more eventful than present day car journeys.

"When we used to go in and out with the pony and trap we had one pony who was very reliable and one who wasn't so good and there was an old boy who had two sticks or even one crutch and one stick who wasn't too mobile and my mother always used to employ him, she used to tie the pony up to a lamp post and then she used to employ him to watch her. I often thought, well if she did anything, what he could have done with his one crutch and his one stick, I can't imagine! The road to Bideford was narrower then from Forest Hill to Ford House, the cliff sort of overhung you and of course it was much quieter. We had a car as well but when petrol was rationed, the ration was so small it just wasn't worth it".

The car now rules everyone's life in the village. It is so easy to leave Littleham in the pursuit of amusement, work, shopping and companionship that no one looks to the community to provide these things anymore. There is a greater range of activities available but that sense of togetherness, of being a member of a close-knit community has gone, perhaps for ever.

Chapter Thirteen

A Sense of Community

"We all got on pretty well together in the old days, the fact that there weren't as many people, then obviously people knew each other better. The number of people who live in Littleham now, I don't know half of them, yet when I went to school I could tell you the name of every person in every house but I couldn't tell you now. And because there's more people, more families, more houses, there is more individuality. I mean you had the Beer family, the Stevens family, the Cook family and the Brends and the Hearns and that wiped out three quarters of the population. I mean just here there was the Cooks at Council Cottage, the Cooks at number nine Mount Pleasant and the Cooks at number one. Then you had the Beers at number five, number seven, Hall-sannery Farm and West Ashbridge and they were all related. Then the Stevens and the Beers were related and Charlie Wood at Dunn Farm, his mother was a Beer. So if you go back far enough, not only did they all know each other, they were also related to each other which doesn't necessarily mean you get on I know but you knew how they would react to a certain problem. You didn't have to go and say, do you mind if I do this or that, you knew. Then there was the poorer type of person like Charlie Batten for instance who flittered all his money, well I don't want to degrade them but they were of no consequence, if someone put up a bullock house Charlie Batten would be the last one to say well, you haven't got planning permission. These things just went on in these villages."

When Alan Marshall told me this, I realised why I had felt isolated from the rest of the community in my early days in the village. I was not part of the extended family which made up the village, I was a stranger, unknown, unpredictable, who had to be observed for several years before being accepted. No doubt it would have taken longer had my family not been known to many people. It is often said that people in isolated communities are suspicious and unfriendly to outsiders, it is a standing joke in North Devon that a newcomer will still be considered a "furriner" after twenty years. This has often been used as a criticism of North Devonians but this suspicion of strangers has to be seen in context, it is because village communities were so small and so closely knit, everyone's habits and foibles so well known that any newcomer, by contrast was as unknown as might be a visitor from another planet. He would be approached with caution but also with hospitality, those who claim to find North Devonians unfriendly have usually earned this attitude.

Winifred Johns moved into the community in the thirties and has seen many changes over the years. Had she found people welcoming?

"Lovely! More friendly than they are today may I say. I mean, well young and old, they differ don't they. They live their lives and I live mine sort of thing. I mean we're all friendly but we don't visit now like we used to, not that tap on the door, how be 'ee this morning sort of thing. You'd leave your doors open then. I've been to town many a time and left the door unlocked, now we won't go down the garden unless it's locked up. Oh it's a shame i'n'it! Well you don't know who's parading around today do you, there's so much damage done everywhere.

I've walked through Littleham and not a soul do I see! And I mean at one time you'd see them out sweeping up outside or talking to their next door neighbour, you don't see it today. Whether it's younger ones and they're out to work, that I don't know but it's dead! And of course there again, years ago they'd have their doors open but now everybody got their doors shut. You never know who's going to walk in, I think that makes an awful lot of difference."

When everything was known about everyone in the village, there could be complete trust.

"If there was a knock at the door you'd never go, you'd just shout come in, you took it for granted it was someone you knew."

The population has changed so rapidly over the last ten years that a knock at the door is now more likely to be a stranger than a friend. Opportunities for meeting neighbours are limited and even the children are isolated since the village school closed and they attend a variety of different schools in the area. Alan Marshall again:

"There were no bus routes in the village when I started school, none at all. Some people would make the effort to go in on a Saturday but others that didn't have any transport would rely on the door to door salesmen all the time, they'd never leave the village. To take the opposite extreme, someone like Charlie Batten, if he had a pound in his pocket he'd be in every night because there was no pub you see. I think perhaps if the school had closed later or the pub had opened earlier and the two had overlapped one another, the focal point might have carried on from the school to the pub. It's not a real village pub, it's no one's fault but it opened twenty years too late and all the characters had gone,

Jack Clements and Charlie Batten would have been in there all the time and then others would have gone in and it would have carried on."

The Post Office provided a focal point until it closed in 1987. It was first run by Maud Badcock who still lives in the same little cottage which housed the Post Office for thirty five years. She rarely leaves her house now and since so many of the older inhabitants have left the village, receives few visitors, in contrast to the days when there was always someone climbing the steps to the front door.

"1903 I was born, eighty six this year. 1925 I moved to Littleham, married and came right out here. My husband was a gardener in to Bideford, different places, nurseries. Us didn't know anyone in Littleham but there weren't many houses going to suit your pocket, didn't give a lot for it. I didn't go out to work, I had the children you see and us had plenty to do. In fact there weren't the work about then, people had girls living indoor, there weren't houses here really, they all had their own, down at Crossways they had them indoors and you know, lived indoors.

I had the Post Office in '35 and I had it thirty five years, I done the post round for several years, I can't tell you when I started it, when my husband was took bad 'cause he used to do it, he died in '47. There wasn't no Post Office before, people had to go to Bideford. In they days the postman had to carry stamps and also he was supposed to bring your medicine to 'ee, they had to, couldn't refuse you. Our postman used to be yer and away from this post office at half past seven, I had to sort them then take them all, all down to Woods, down to Gillespie's all down Scratchyface and the other postman used to go next door to there but I still had to go! If they were bills I'd keep 'em! I took two dogs with me, regular. When the snow was here the postman couldn't bring the post up, you had to fetch it from Orleigh Mill, done that several times, had the snow so bad they couldn't come up the hill. The post office was open every day and Saturdays up 'til one o'clock. I had a shop, sold everything, cheese, ham, you had to do all sorts to get a bit of money. The wages wasn't nothing really you see. You'd always have someone in and out you know, they'd come from around, different places. Done very well really, sweets, sweets for the children.

People were in and out, I used to see a lot more than what I do now! I used to write their letters for 'em, and read 'em. A lot of people couldn't write nor read you see. Granny Jollow couldn't read nor write, every time she had to write to her daughter or son I had to write that, sometimes they'd be a bit sharp! Mrs Brend couldn't write, they wasn't bound to go to school you see, years ago. Charlie Batten couldn't write, I used to have to sign his book for him.

Everyone was friendly, never had a row with anybody, they was good people really, all of them. In they days, there was Granny Jollow and

Granny Moyse and they like ruled the village, didn'em. Everybody respected 'em, they was very old people. Granny Moyse worked for Parson Hawker out at Morwenstow, you know that very famous parson? And 'er worked for him when 'er was nine year old, 'er told me all about it. And then there was Granny Jollow and you used to respect 'em, didn'ee? Do everything for 'em, fetch the milk for 'em, give 'em things, used to fetch the milk for 'em for threepence a week. Get their cans before school, go down there, Middle Langdon, fetch the milk for 'em. Twouldn't do now, would it!"

The benefits of living in a close-knit community are obvious. But what of those who through character or circumstance found it hard to conform to the rather narrow demands of the inhabitants? Were they tolerated or was the pressure to conform so great that those who could not conform were forced to leave? I asked Charlie Cook whether many girls had to get married in those days.

"Well not a lot I don't think, not really, no. They seemed to go out just for the pleasure of company's sake, not anything else. Mind there were some, some of course. There was a poor old girl went throwed 'erself in the well up Apps, drowned 'erself, they say her was like that, that was about 1920 I think it was, I remember it quite well. Course anything like that, to the older people it was an awful thing, an awful thing for they. What they'd say now to all the photos in the paper, my, 'tis nothing but naked woman every week, they'd be disgusted. My old Granny! In fact my mother would, her's shocked her would be. Yep, 'twas a very bad thing if anything happened like that, 'tisn't like it is today, nobody don't take no notice of it now."

Gertie Beer also remembered this particular suicide.

"Annie Baglow drowned herself up at Apps, she was pregnant you see. Her father went down the well to take the poor girl up, he went down this great big deep well on a rope, it was awful sad. The poor dear, it worried her to death, what she must have went through."

Her grave can be found in the churchyard, the headstone slightly obscured by tall flowering grasses. No flowers are placed there now but early purple orchids push through the turf each spring. The inscription reads:

In Loving Memory
of
Annie Baglow
Who died Jan. 17th 1916
aged 26 years.
Art thou weary, art thou languid,
Art thou sore distrest?
"Come to me", saith one, "and coming,
Be at rest."

She is remembered now with sympathy and sorrow but it may be that had she not killed herself, she would be remembered with quite different emotions.

Those who strayed beyond the social mores could not expect complete tolerance but there was room for eccentricity, every village has its characters and Littleham was no exception. Everywhere I went, I would hear the name of Charlie Batten so I started to ask who he was and I found that everyone had a story to tell about him.

"Charlie Batten was known in Bideford as Littleham Charlie, he just used to live for his beer. He lost his eye trimming hedges, that was really neglect, he got a scratch in his eye from a bramble or something and he just wouldn't go to the doctor and it got worse and worse until eventually he lost his eye. It didn't disillusion him, when I first left school I used to pick potatoes with him and he used to say he got two pounds a week pension for this eye and he used to reckon he could see well enough with one eye and the two pounds would buy several pints of beer! He was quite happy!"

"Oh he was a case he was! But he wouldn't harm anyone you know, no he was a harmless old chap. He used to do anything, he used to work all around, he was a good worker, a very good worker. He wouldn't let beer or anything like that interfere with his work, he had his beer after he left work, he used to like it I know!"

"Charlie Batten? Oh my word! He lived in number two, by himself when his mother died. He was ever so comical but he'd never do nobody no harm. He was an absolute character! He used to drink and that, terrible. He was known to go around three times around Upcott Hills to try to get home of a night, come up Upcott Hills, down Wagon Road, round again, he's done it three times before it gets to the morning and then he'd be getting a bit more sober and he'd gradually make it home. He's been into town three times in one day before, you see he was in the infantry and twenty miles marching was nothing to Charlie! He'd always have the front door open and if it was a cold day he'd have the fire up the chimney and the door open! He was shell-shocked you see, couldn't be shut in. He never sawed no sticks, just stick em' in the fire and let 'em burn, have a big stick right across the room and burn a piece off and a piece off. Black! He was black. Some new people came up to him and said where does so and so live and Charlie said, next to Georgie Wise, just said next to Georgie Wise and walked right on! So this man, 'e come in to me and he said, do you know where Georgie Wise lives! I'll never forget that, 'e was a case, old Charlie!"

"Charlie was a very proud man you see, and 'e bought a new shirt and it was Monday morning and 'e went down Littleham Hill doing water tabling and anyway about ten o'clock it came on to rain. Well Charlie said 'tis a pity, – well 'e didn't say a pity but I mustn't swear, – 'e said 'tis a pity to get me shirt wet 'e said, so 'e took 'ees shirt off and worked all day in the rain, put 'ees shirt in the rabbit's hole. When 'e went back about five o'clock the rain 'ad got in and all the mud had come in all over 'ees shirt! So 'e wouldn't wear 'ees shirt when 'twas raining, said 'tis a pity to get 'n wet, worked all day with just 'ees – nothing at all on!

Us never called him Charlie, it was always Mr Batten out of respect. He was a farm labourer, used to work for Mr Mills quite a bit. Another thing Charlie used to do, 'e used to go thrashing, farm after farm and 'e always had the hardest job to do, the trusser that was it, very dusty job and you couldn't see Charlie's eyes after a day of it. But 'e'd do day after day of it and 'e'd do two man's work in a day. But he was everyone's friend, Charlie. He was good-natured he was. He got the Bronze Star. He was gassed too 'e was."

"Charlie Batten, he was a character, he was a bit strange! My father used to employ him a bit sometimes, and my husband. He used to go out and do the rough work you see and he used to go out and get a bit wet, get his feet wet and he'd come in and say in this whiney old voice, "Missis" he'd say "have you got a pair of socks you could let me have 'cos me socks are awful wet". Oh he'd be in a pitiful state and you'd have to go and find him a pair somewhere! I've heard them say he used to drink an awful lot and when he came home from town sometimes he'd fall out with his bicycle and by the time he got home his bicycle would be in parts, he was so drunk to ride it he fell out with it! They used to laugh about him!"

"He used to go around, casual work sort of thing and he used to come a bit before Christmas to our place, Got any work Maister? He'd get an extra pound or something, he knew he'd get a better Christmas if he came then. He was a nice old boy. He always went to town every Saturday night, had his drink. He left his bike down the bottom of Upcott Hills and then Sunday morning he'd have to go and pick up the bike! He couldn't get up the hills with'n, so he would cuss and swear to the old bike and chuck'n in the hedge! I've been walking up those hills, bin to pictures or something, and you'd yer footsteps and 'twould be, Wye up! Charlie Batten 'twould be, 'e'd always say wye up, frighten you to death!"

"He always used to play the mouth organ up at the dances and sing "To be a Farmer's Boy"!

"Charlie was in his seventies when he died, '71. They collected for his burial because he hadn't got nothing, he was going to be buried on the parish. Nobody refused, we got enough money for a good funeral and to pay off all his debts. The church was packed and the Rector, he gave a wonderful address on princes and palaces, he said well Charlie, he never lived in a palace, you never seen anything like it in your life! but he definitely was a prince. Us miss'n though, Charlie. Oh us have had some characters yer!"

Another name which was often mentioned was Jack Clements.

"Littleham was well endowed with characters! Jack Clements was an ex-Naval bloke who lived in Old Moor Cottages, the one on the right. He lived with his mother, he was quite a character. He's rather difficult to describe, he wasn't a very clean man to put it politely, he would have been about fifty at this time, in about 1948 say, he must have been about as old as the century. After his mother died he let the house go, the garden got overgrown, the house got in a helluva state inside, he used to keep a couple of cats and it was filthy. After a while there was just a path between the undergrowth to get to the front door, inside was terrible, we used to sneak in to look through the windows. Being an ex-Naval man he used to get some sort of pension and most of his money went on beer and he used to nick his firewood from the Rectory. Every afternoon without fail you'd see Jack coming up Rectory Drive with a stick on his shoulder, been down to pinch his night's firing!"

"Old man Clements, he was the head gardener at Rectory, I can mind them when I was a boy. Mother and father were very strict and saved money but Jack had been in the Navy, well he spent it all. He was so dirty as they were clean. Edward Stevens saw him picking eggs out th' 'edge, putting them in his pocket so he gave him a slap, broke the eggs! And he used to help hisself to swedes from the field."

When I first moved to Littleham I used to see an old man whose clothes made him look as though he had just walked off a film set, a film depicting village life in Edwardian times perhaps. He wore loose corduroy breeches, gaiters, a waistcoast, and walked with a stiff-legged gait, so bow-legged that he looked as if he had spent most of his life on horseback. This was Sid Wise, the last remaining member of his family. He died before I had got to know him well enough to exchange more than a brief greeting. Alan Marshall used to pass him every morning on his way to school.

"Harold, Sid and May Wise lived at Chapel Cottage, Sid was the postman. When I was walking to school I always used to know whether I was early or late as to how far down Scratchyface I was when I met Sid, as I was going up, Sid would be coming down. I can see him now going to his pocket and lifting out his pocket watch and saying, in good time this morning, or something like that."

It seems most houses in Littleham have a story attached to them. Alan remembered the people who used to live in the houses which nestle in the valley at the foot of Scratchyface Lane.

"Summerhill and Summerhall, they both used to be called Summerhill. In the top one there was a Miss Peete, a district nurse and she had, I suppose you would call her a servant woman living with her called Alice Williams, both of those were right characters really. Miss Peete was quite an educated person but not the cleanest of nurses and the house wasn't the cleanest of houses. Alice Williams was a quaint old soul, she used to wear these laced up boots and you'd see her trotting into town taking very short steps, dressed completely in black with a black straw hat, one of these tall hats made out of straw. Most inoffensive little woman, hardly used to say anything to you. There was a fellow lived with them in the other half, though it wasn't really subdivided, and that was Jack Slader. Jack Slader and his father before him, he ran a carpenter's business, a wheelwright's it would have been. I'd pass him on Scratchyface and although he knew me, he'd never speak. He hung himself in his own workshop down there."

It is hard to believe that the next generation of villagers will produce such characters, but there are still some of the old ones left. Glennie can still be seen sitting in his wheelchair at Crossways waving to passing cars, though his greetings are returned less often these days. Most of the newcomers to the village, embarrassed by their inability to understand his answers, do not attempt to speak to him more than once and indeed his speech seems to have become less clear as if through lack of practice. He rarely makes the effort to wheel himself up to the village now that so many of his old friends have left and it is difficult to see what the future holds for him.

"Glennie was much better in those days than what he is today although he was never quite normal. At school he could just about sign his name and pick out a few words. He worked on Boundstone Farm for a while when he left school and he used to drive a tractor and he used to ride his bike. His first catastrophe was when he was cycling down Littleham Hill and the mudguard came off and jammed his wheel up and he went back over and hit his head. As far as Glen was concerned that was the start of his big problems, he lost his speech and when he eventually got his speech back it wasn't as clear as before and it never had been very clear. Then his other catastrophe was in 1975 when he fell off a ladder and paralysed himself. We don't exactly know how bad he's paralysed, I have actually seen him stand but it's very difficult to know. It's a sad state of affairs with his mother the way she is and Glennie so incapacitated, she won't have any help."

"When Glen had his accident they took him off to hospital and they said he would be back about half past four and that was in May and he never came out til November. What a time her had with him! (His mother). Every day she went to see him in hospital in Exeter, someone in the village would take her every day. And there wasn't a bit of sense when she got there, her was always wanting to know what he was having to eat, she spent all the time asking what he'd had and he couldn't tell her and she'd say one thing and he'd say no and when she left she didn't know what he'd had for dinner! Oh us have seen some times with him! Course there was a time when Glen could do things, he'd help people, do a bit of work. He ought to walk of course, he used to walk but now he's happy riding round in that chair. At one time he'd go as far as Abbotsham Cross in that chair. Do you remember that time when he got hold of the policeman's hat, he was stopping everybody, directing traffic! Poor old Glennie, us have seen some times with him."

It is people like Glennie, the handicapped and the old, who suffer most when community life diminishes and amenities are lost.

Strangers in a small village have always been the subject of much interest. Even these days visitors rarely find their way to Littleham, the narrow winding lanes are enough to deter all but the most adventurous tourists and these find little to interest them unless they find their way down to the church. How much more isolated it must have been before cars became so numerous. Any visitor to the village was bound to be the subject of comment and speculation. One farmer remembered the less welcome visitors.

"You'd have a tramp would come around and come in for a cup of tea. If they came into the farm well they were given a bit of bread and brawn or bread and cream or something. They used to say, well you shouldn't do that cos they leave a sign for the next one. Then there used to be someone used to go around with a bicycle selling oranges. Then the poor old paper chap, he was deaf's a post. I can mind when I was a boy he'd got like a two stroke motor bike went along put, put, put. He'd have a job to pull away so us boys would go out and hold the back part so he couldn't pull away!

We had a chap once looked a bit suspicious and someone said, bet he's going up on your hay tonight! So of course then I was worried he'd be going up there smoking so when I came back I climbed up on the rick. When I got up on top the rick there was a peek, so I got up walking around the hay rick sticking this peek in. All of a sudden this feller jumped up and I didn't know who was going to run, me or the feller! But he cleared off and went back to another farm. Next morning the other farmer came along and stirred him out, farmer up the road, he said, he took a peek for me he said!"

It might be imagined that war would have little effect on an isolated village far from the nearest bombing but the net of war was spread wide and everyone had their memories to tell. Charlie Cook was too young to fight in the First World War, but old enough to remember it.

"I was about nine year old when the First War started, I remember it very well. There used to be an old postman came along here mornings, on the way to school we used to ask him what the war news was because there weren't no television nor wireless so he'd tell us a certain place had been bombed or something like that. There was two killed from the village."

Farmers did not always have an easy time.

"During the First World War, Granfer was a horse dealer so he bought a lot of horses for France. When me dad had to go in the Army, me Grandfather said, someone has got to pay. So he made sure, he bought horses and sold to France to pay for his son having to leave the farm. Often he would come home with a dozen horses and sell within a few days to France. Me Father, being in the Army got friendly with an officer and was able to tell dad what contacts to get hold of to buy the horses."

Everyone was affected by the Second World War. I asked whether it was difficult to manage with rationing.

"Well, we thought it was but we weren't so bad off as they were in the towns, not really. We'd got our own vegetables and farmers was glad to get rid of their butter and their cream, butter half a crown a pound. We had some chickens, we started off with five hens and those five hens paid for the wire netting and the shed that we built up, in eighteen months. Eggs were about ninepence a dozen! We bought some more and I think the most we had were about thirty and then culled out the cockerels you knaw. We managed very well on our coupons, what we couldn't have we'd go without. I don't think people in the country did too badly, not really. I mean in the towns they had to be a bit more strict with rationing but of course there was always those that wanted more than their share."

"We weren't rationed, just jam and sugar and you see we had our own butter and milk. Then we always killed a pig twice a year and salted the meat and that lasted us a long while, ham and bacon and things like that. It was tight for some people who hadn't got anything coming in but we grew all our own vegetables so you could make dishes up then, 'tisn't like you've got nothing. We kept fowls as well, we had eggs."

"Blackouts, us had blackouts of course, had to black out our windows and that. And the rationing was tight, shouldn't like to go back to that again. We were rationed for butter and things like that, there wasn't no one making butter round here you see. We'd have a rabbit sometimes, Mr Mills 'ud give 'ee a rabbit, shilling he'd say, lovely rabbit for a shilling! Well you'd be delighted with 'ee. Now I wouldn't look at 'em, now that they've had that old stuff."

The Home Guard is the source of some amusement, in true Dad's Army fashion. Charlie told me of his experiences.

"There was the Home Guard here in Littleham of course, Major Atkinson was in charge of that, we used to go to Bucks Mills for our headquarters. We used to go there one night a week, stay up there all night and take it in turns to keep watch in twos. One night we saw the fish, the scales shining up and thought it was Gerry coming so we gave some kind of warning! Another time we were on an exercise up Parkham Woods, supposed to be tracking down Gerry who they said was holed up there somewhere. Well it started to rain and we got fed up with this so someone said, there he goes! up towards the pub! So we all went to the pub after Gerry!"

At one time it looked as if Littleham might see some real action.

"In the Second World War the Army commandeered Apps Cottage and put tins of biscuits in it for an emergency. Then there was two families of evacuees there for a time. When the Army came through at the beginning of the War, I can mind seeing the Army from one end of the lane to the other in training. They stayed at Apps, they slept in the barns and the officers slept in the cottage. They stayed about a fortnight and then they moved on. They was training you see, you looked down the lane and you saw soldiers all down through the old lane. Goodness me, well we wondered what was coming, true."

It was the arrival of the evacuees which had the greatest affect on the village. At Heale House, Vi McDougall had plenty of room for visitors.

"The first lot of evacuees came from Peckham Rye. They, the billeting people, they just took account of the size of the house, I suppose rather like it is in Russia. But they didn't give any thought as to whether anyone had beds and bedding for that many, I mean if they didn't I suppose they had to go and buy it. And so it was decreed that we had room for six. And then they arrived at the village hall and my mother went up and she said it was rather as she'd always imagined a slave market would be, trying to pick out the strongest ones! So initially we had five boys and a girl. We always imagined they liked being here but I don't know if they did really. But I think they enjoyed the animals you see and I don't think they sort of missed the town. Some parents came and I don't think they liked it and then these children, their parents would come down every now and again, suddenly, because they didn't want you to know they were coming, to see how cruel you were being to them and, well they couldn't imagine anyone living in the sticks like that! And then as well as them we had two elderly aunts, well no, great aunts they were really, who'd been bombed out of their house in Streatham and of course they were real Victorians. And so they were there too, so there was quite a lot of us one way and another. The evacuees, they ate with Dorothy and Mary and we ate elsewhere.

You knew Mrs Lyle in the village I expect, did you? She had two evacuees, twins, Peter and Paul. Well she kept her house absolutely immaculate and everything was very nice and Peter and Paul used to fight and then one day they fought and they made one another's noses bleed and they put their hands to their noses you see and then they did this all over the wall! And that was just too much for poor Mrs Lyle! So she said she just couldn't bear it any more and so it was thought that perhaps it would be better if the twins were split up. And so one of the original six, its parents must have taken it back I suppose and we had one of those. And I must say we never had any trouble so I suppose it was just that they probably used to enjoy fighting really.

Well then eventually they all went back and America came into the war and the Americans requistioned quite a lot of houses on the front at Instow. And what is now the Commodore Hotel was owned by some people called Bourne and they were told they had to get out. And of course you see a lot of people had come to this part of the world because of it being safe and it wasn't all that easy to get places. So Mr and Mrs Bourne and their two teenage children, we agreed that they should have part of the house and do for themselves and everything. So they came and used up a bit of room and then also a Mrs Johnson came and had another part. So when the next lot of evacuees came which was from Bristol, by then we were full, so we didn't have any in the next wave."

It was on the village school that the arrival of the evacuees had the greatest influence, but that event came comparatively late in the history of Littleham School.

Chapter Fourteen

The Village School

Littleham and Landcross School was built in 1877 for ninety children at a cost of £600. It is thought that there was a dame school in the village before this time but obviously no information can be obtained on this from living memory. Charlie Cook started school in 1908.

"I went to school when I was three year old, I don't remember much about that! It was a very nice school, there was a hundred, over a hundred there sometimes. Well you see you come to take eighteen in two houses, it soon mounts up dunnit! There was several teachers, the last one was Miss Rowe, there was a Miss Carter, there was a Miss Ellis. If you did anything, you'd have to hold out your hand, you'd get the cane, used to have the cane back in they days! I've never had homework to do, that was the funny thing about it, me daughter and son, they used to bring home this homework but we never used to have to do any of it."

It was on the question of punishment that memory proved most vivid; one wonders what the present generation of schoolchildren will remember most about their schooldays now that corporal punishment has been abolished. I asked a farmer what he remembered about school.

"What do I remember about school? Wondering when I was going to get home again! They used to let us help do the gardening occasionally, that was always a treat if we could get out in the garden, it was a break from the lessons.

I mind my Father (born 1897) saying, one day when he was naughty he had to stand in a corner and hold a dozen slates above his head. So he decided he wasn't going to do that much longer so he let them all fall!

I had the cane a few times, you had to hold your hand out and have three daps with the cane. If you whipped your hand away you had one more! I can mind telling me father, oh I've had the cane, he said don't come home telling me that or you'll have another one! In his day they were a lot stricter. I think it done me good."

William started school in 1905 and his memories of eighty four years ago were as vivid as if they had happened yesterday.

"The families were so big and they used to take from Landcross and Whitehall and on the other side down to Knowle, well there was about twenty children used to come up from Knowle, that's down by Jennets you see. Miss Rowe was the headmistress and her sister was the second in charge and they was as different as chalk and cheese really. Well they taught us very well in reading, writing and arithmetic, we didn't have any special subjects but we was always very good taught in that. There was never no examinations nor nothing like that, you just went to school and you had the cane if you didn't behave yourself. We sat all along at a desk, you didn't have separate desks, well they used to call them forms, as you progressed you'd go over in the front form, or the back form, I forget which way it did used to work. But as you progressed you used to come up. If you misbehaved or you were talking to your boyfriend next door, you'd be brought out and you'd have to sit at the table as a sort of punishment.

We used to walk up to school, there was a bell they used to ring at school. The boys' toilets were up on the left and the girls' up on the right, well up around the boys' there was a space, as you progressed you was allowed to till these as flower beds you see, we used to till a flower bed there. The Rector would come up and give you a scripture lesson. In those days, the girls, if they met the Rector out in the road they had to curtsey to him, my, what a change, i'n'it! Now there isn't a Rector there at all.

We used to take our midday meal and if you had a special friend you'd swop your lunch, you'd eat his and he'd eat yours. We'd go over in the village and in the end house, before you come to the one on its own, there was an old lady called Mrs Sheenery, she was a bit of a notorious sort of person but I didn't know much about her. Well one day we were over in the village and there was a pigeon stood on the wall and one of the boys upped with a stone and threw at this pigeon, he missed the pigeon and went right through Mother Sheenery's window! My, we were back to Littleham School faster than you saw anything in your life!

I used to have the cane with the rest of them you know but not too bad. Miss Rowe herself, it took a lot before she would cane you but her sister Mrs Chubb, didn't take much to upset her. There was a boy there called Ernie Clements and you had to hold out your hand you see to have this cane, so as he saw the cane coming down, he'd whip his hand back. So one day she brought the cane down then whipped it up and caught him right up under the nose! All of us didn't know how to stop from laughing!

Before they built the school house, the schoolmistress used to live in the bottom Red Cottage. When we were little there was what we used to call the big boys, the thirteen and fourteens, it was surprising how big they used to look when you're small, the big girls used to sit up one side, well you'd picture them almost like grown up when you're small you see. Well anyway, one day when there was a lot of rain and there was a lot of water going down the road, there was a gutter, a drain outside Miss Rowe's place, I don't know if it's still there, the boys went down in the dinner hour and choked this gutter and she couldn't come up to open the school! That was the good old days! In the top one there was a Miss Martin used to keep a little shop, you could go down and have a pennyworth of sherbet or anything else you wanted. Wicked boys really, some of us were, we weren't all so good as perhaps you might think! Now Miss Martin, you'd come into her shop and she'd have all these sweets on the corner of the table, she'd be sitting down the back and ask what you want. She used to keep some things in the window, as you passed down there you could see it, I don't know if you've been down there but anyway I dare say it's changed now. But you'd ask for a pennyworth of something in the window, while she went in after it, you'd help yourself to a few licorice allsorts! Shameful really!"

Most village schools have a wide catchment area and Littleham was no exception, taking children from scattered farms and cottages up to two miles from the village. There was no school transport in those days of course so many had a long walk before and after the school day. I had always imagined that this might be rather pleasant in fine weather, children would have the company of their peers, plenty of opportunities for adventures and the chance to observe and appreciate their environment. My illusions were shattered by Gertie Beer's daughter, Gwen Barrow.

"Until my brother was old enough to start school I walked from Hallsannery Farm to the school on my own and they were lonely narrow rough roads. I dreaded meeting a steam engine and threshing machine, it was usually on the way home from school after they had finished a day's threshing corn on a local farm. There were very few passing places and I remember running to the nearest gateway for them to pass, they were such big noisy things, it was really frightening for a little child. Then my father used to keep a bull at Hallsannery and there always used to be somebody driving cows along the lane to the farm, 'twas horrible, they used to be so wild sometimes! Then there used to be the odd tramp with a perambulator or wheelbarrow with their worldly things in, I used to be frightened of them. At Apps there was the slaughterhouse and you'd pass the gate where the poor old sheep were penned up and two men slaughtering away like mad, stunning them and cutting their throats, then they'd put them on a wheelbarrow and take them in to hang them up, 'twas horrible the things I used to see on the way to school!"

There were other hazards for the children who lived outside the village.

"The children who used to walk long distances used to bring packed lunches in bags and hang them up in the porch on pegs where they hung their clothes. Sometimes a stray dog would arrive and steal their food and then the teachers used to take pity on them and give them something to eat!"

Gwen's sister Christine Luxton, who attended the school in the forties, remembers children bringing raw potatoes to school which the infant teacher, Miss Kingdom, used to put in the bottom of the tortoise stove to bake for lunch. This tortoise stove seemed to terrorise the school, when the wind was blowing from a certain direction it used to belch out thick black smoke and all the windows would have to be opened, however cold the weather outside. This seems to have been a long-standing problem.

At a Meeting of the Managers. Schoolroom. December 11th 1905. Resolved that Mr J. Cock (Builder) Bideford should put cowls on each chimney pot of the School to prevent the smoke coming down into the Schoolrooms.

In wet weather some children would arrive at school soaked to the skin and their clothes would be draped around the stove to dry, they would steam and Gwen Barrow remembers feeling quite overpowered by the smell of drying socks. If the children managed to withstand all this, there was a further danger, large brown jars of cod liver oil and malt kept on a high shelf, two teaspoons to be given daily to thin delicate children. The water supply presented another problem.

At a meeting of the managers. March 20th 1905. A letter was produced by Mr A.J. Heywood from the district Sanitory Inspector respecting the water in the well of the school, stating it was unfit for the children to drink.

June 20th 1910. A letter from the Medical Officer of Health, with reference to the water in the school well which stated that the supply had become contaminated and the necessity of the scholars not drinking the water.

In July 1910 the sale of a well at Apps was offered for £10.

September 29th 1913. The water at the new well having failed to supply the School and the Schoolhouse with water, the disused well had to be resorted to and the Pump of same being out of order , the Correspondent was instructed to have it repaired as soon as possible.

At a quarterly meeting of the Managers. 26th October 1942. Reported that the scholars would not drink the water at the school. Resolved that the County be informed and asking them to deal with the matter.

Gwen Barrow again:

"A dentist used to attend to inspect teeth and the school doctor used to visit to examine us, always on the lookout for T.B. or consumption as it was called then. The school nurse used to be a frequent visitor as there used to be lots of children suffering from head lice. We used to play ball games, hopscotch and hoops in the playground. The playground was just rough stones and children often used to fall down and graze their legs badly."

21st January 1936. At a quarterly meeting of the Managers.
The managers again decided to make application for something to be done to improve the surface of the bottom yard which is in a very rough state.

It was not long before there were more serious problems to consider.
25th October 1939. At a quarterly meeting of the Managers.
Safety of the children during an Air Raid. The Chairman said he thought this matter could be left to the discretion of the Head Mistress, who would carry out the County's instructions as far as she was able, and this was agreed to. The Chairman considered the narrow road outside the school gate, with its fairly high banks, would provide a natural shelter from anything but a direct hit, and it was decided that this course be adopted if the necessity arose. Closing school earlier during the winter, to enable the caretaker to do her cleaning before the blackout, was left to the Head Mistress to act as she thought necessary.

Gwen remembers the arrival of evacuee children causing a great upheaval.

"When the evacuee children came from Peckham in the war, they were very rough and we local ones used to clique together because they were very rough and they were fightable some of them. They were big children and stronger than the Littleham children. There was quite a trouble with them taking things, you know, stealing but I wouldn't hold it against them because poor children, no doubt they were under a lot of stress and strain. There were the three rooms at the school and it was overcrowded!"

29th July 1940.
The Head Mistress reported that the evacuees were settling down at the school.

Gwen's brother, Horace Beer.

"The thing that stands out in my mind is when the evacuees came. We were just a little country school, a little close-knit school, and I always remember the morning we got up there and there must have been an extra hundred children there like. There were children everywhere and they were having lessons out in the porch. As far as us Devonshire children were concerned it totally upset our education in a way, children had to be divided into age groups and some of us were being taught stuff we'd covered a twelvemonth back, I was appalled that some of the children of our own age group couldn't read. It was true that some of us Devon children, well some weren't quite right in the head but I was appalled that some of the evacuees, intelligent children, couldn't read. Then some of them were rough, there were numerous fights as they tried to assert themselves, we resented them really, there were fights between the girls as well! It was cruel really, poor little things. One or two tried to make a run back to London once, they got as far as Ilfracombe I think, they was headed a little bit wrong! Poor little devils. As time went on we did mix with them a bit more, but initially there was some nasty moments up there!"

October 26h 1941.

Reported that Miss Raynor, evacuee teacher, had been ordered a complete rest.

"Some of the evacuees were very keen on collecting birds' eggs and it was nothing but a racket really, some of us Devonshire boys used to make up some fancy name for these eggs and they would buy it! We used to collect a lot of waste paper during the war and Littleham School won the cup for that, we were at an advantage because we used to get the waste paper from Mr Saunders down Orleigh Mills."

26th October 1942.

It was reported that the bi-monthly Hilton Cup awarded for salvage collecting had been won by the School for September.

"We used to have these savings weeks during the War, we used to have Air Week and Victory Week and you were encouraged to bring an extra sixpence from your savings, I remember some officer would come around and whip the children up a bit, that sixpence would buy a bullet, he'd say, and that bullet would kill a German! Terrible when you come to think of it, sixpence to a kill a German!

A favourite pastime was smashing the insulators up on the wires, we'd take a shot at those."

October 27th 1941.

The Correspondant was directed to write to the Head Teacher requesting a warning be given the children of the danger of climbing the Telegraph Poles. It was stated that this was a practice that was prevalent in the village at the present time..

"Then another thing was sabotaging the village pump, we'd take a nut off the top or something then every now and then the policeman would come to sort us out! When we saw the policeman come across the yard, we always knew someone was in trouble! He'd come across from Buckland on his bike and you'd see him come stalking across the yard and you'd think, oh who is it this time. I remember I had great plans to climb the roof and ring the bell but then I went to Grammar School and I never did get back to do it.

Father had the contract to supply the school with milk and Gwen and I used to hate that because we had to carry these damn cans of milk to school with us and carry the empty ones home. We'd get so fed up we used to fall out, we'd say one had to carry the cans so far, then we'd have a row and drop them in the road and walk on a long way and one of us would have to give way and go back after them! Sometimes we were driven to school but we always had to carry the empty ones home.
25th January 1946.

Reported that Mr E. Beer wished to give up supplying the milk to the School. It was recommended that Mrs Stevens of Boundstone Farm be asked if she would supply and also to ask the permission of the County for the Dining Centre Helper to deliver the milk to the School.

"We used to go on these nature walks and my auntie, Mrs Stevens was very keen on having an aquarium so we used to go down Edge Mills and catch these little fish, well then we had to look after the aquarium and change the water and that. I didn't fancy that too much so I went down to my grandmother's pond, Littleham pond, and caught a newt to put in, I remember my auntie saying, what a rare specimen! And I knew what he was going to do, within hours he ate the lot! So that saved that bother!"

Alan Marshall started school in 1947 and recalled his days there with a mixture of pleasure and disgust.

"When I started school I think there was five of us started together, this was before the Education Act obviously of '48 so the seniors were there. There were two teachers there, Mrs Stevens was the headmistress and Miss Olive Kingdom was the other teacher, she lived at the Tollhouse at the bottom of Scratchyface. She was quite an elderly spinster, or she seemed elderly in those days, thinking about it she must have been something in the region of fifty years of age. She taught the younger ones, up to the age of about ten and then as time ran on, in 1948 the Education Act put paid to the seniors and one teacher was done away with so Mrs Stevens taught the lot. I think when it became a primary school only, there were about twenty four, twenty five children.

I used to walk up Scratchyface to school, all winds and weathers and I didn't used to bat an eyelid really because in those days other children were doing similar kinds of things. All the Wood children walked up from Dunn, the Beers from Hallsannery Farm, the Huxtables from Alverdiscott Farm, the Upton Family lived at Knowle down near Jennets Bridge. In the early days I walked up with Miss Kingdom then when I was about seven a family moved into Spinney Cottage, it was called No Place in those days, and I used to walk up with a girl from there.

We had to be there by half past nine and Mrs Stevens was quite strict. The bell was never used in my day, the bell was there and the trapdoor with the hole where the rope used to hang down but there was no rope. I never remember the bell being rung officially, I think kids would climb up the roof and give it a poke with a stick or summat but that was all!

There was no electric light, there were paraffin lamps although they weren't often lit in lesson time. I think electric lights were put in in about '51. They had electricity in the school for heating water in the kitchen but not lights. There was a well with a pump and the caretaker used to pump the water up into a tank so we had running water. I can remember the inside quite clearly, the piano against the sliding partition and the tortoise stoves. There was a map of the world pinned up.

There was two teaching rooms, the old part of the school was roughly divided into two thirds, one third, and the two thirds was a teaching area and there was sliding glass door and the smaller area was what we used to use as the canteen. Where we used to have the old powdered milk brewed up for lunch break and of course we used to have the midday meal there as well which was brought out from Bideford in insulated steel containers. They used to be brought out in a van which used to arrive at roughly twelve o'clock and used to hang around until we were ready to eat it at around twelve thirty. It was horrible! The food I reckoned was pretty horrible, we used to get a variation but it was all so terrible that I really can't recall what was what. The greens were always yellow and I nicknamed them yellows instead of greens. We used to have that blessed thick custard that you nearly had to cut out of the urn to get it on to your plate and it had a huge thick skin on top of it which put me off custard for the rest of me life actually, I still can't take to it somehow. We used to get various stews, boiled potatoes which were invariably either hard and yellow or black. Terrible stuff and we were made to eat it. The remnants always used to be thrown in a waste bucket and one of the senior boys used to take this old galvanized bucket full of all their rubbish that was left over up through the path past School House and tip it out in Apps Lane for Edward Stevens' pigs and they used to gobble it up in a short space of time. From time to time I used to smuggle what was on my plate into the waste bucket without anyone finding out because it was so terrible! Sago was another thing we used to have, absolutely terrible!

In 1950 Mrs Stevens was ill for a couple of months and we had a supply teacher come in from Bideford. This bloke was a real nutter, he wouldn't teach us nothing, he used to read us stories all day long and we used to soak it up like a sponge, it was a proper job. He would also bring out meccano sets which he'd bought with his own money and we used to have a fine time! I remember one funny occasion. Old Jonesy used to have his dinner separate from us in the main teaching room, whereas Mrs Stevens used to sit at the head of the table to make sure we behaved. From time to time he used to come out and tell us to eat our dinner, say we wouldn't be strong children if we didn't and all this kind of thing. Well one day I was absolutely fed up with this grub and the supervisor had gone up to the back to fill up a coal bucket so I thought, right this is my chance. I'd done this more than once, pick up my plate, whip out through the senior boys' porch , run out into the yard and scrape it out over the school wall for Edward Stevens' chickens, he had about three hundred chickens out there roaming around. Blow me down, there was Jonesy scraping his out over there! I thought, blimey, what a flipping hypocrite! So I waited for him to finish, I tucked myself in around the corner and when he'd dived back in I went out and got rid of mine. Of course the kids were all laughing when I told them, I just got back in time before the supervisor came back. Afterwards we learnt from Granny Lyle who was living in Red Cottages that he done it every day. He was always doing it!

One of the first things I can remember being taught was to tell the time, and I can remember being taught to read a ruler and if we didn't obey Miss Kingdom used to put it across the backs of our hands! At the springtime of the year a suitable afternoon would be chosen and the whole school would go on a nature walk which was quite enjoyable. More often than not we used to walk down to Dunn Farm and see Charlie Wood who was farming at the time and Mrs Stevens used to seek permission to walk through the farmyard and then go on down to Jennetts Reservoir. We'd be instructed to look for frogspawn or toadspawn or newts or this sort of thing and I also remember we used to take a few jars to bring back newts or whatever. We had an aquarium in the school and the boys used to have to look after it and change the water from time to time.

We were always in trouble at school or I was anyhow, for busting a glass in the school windows or something. I know on one occasion we had a spate of making parachutes out of handkerchiefs, we used to knot each corner and load it with some object. I remember getting to school one morning quite early with a big red handkerchief and announcing that I had the one that would stay in the sky the longest, I whizzed it around as fast as I could to whizz it up in the air and instead of going vertical it went horizontal and right through the window into the classroom. I never said a word about it but unfortunately Mrs Stevens noticed the hole in the glass when we were in assembly and eventually I owned up! We used to do all sort of things!

One of Mrs Stevens' favourite punishments if you misbehaved, stand out in the porch, she used to say. You'd go out there and you'd be there for hours sometimes, she'd forget all about you! I know Colin Wood was sent out on one occasion and he must have gone out and told his father about it and he said, boy, if 'er 'adn't got nought better for you to do, next time 'er sends you out you come 'oom cos I'll give 'ee a job! And he did too!

There were no other kids in my immediate area but as I got older I used to come up to the village to see others. There was very little through traffic, really the only people who had cars were the farmers and the, well you wouldn't exactly call them gentry but you know who I mean, there were only two or three apart from the farmers who had cars. We used to do quite a bit of birdsnesting, I don't think we used to abuse it, perhaps just take one from a cluster of four or five. I did have quite a collection of birds' eggs.

When we were out in the playground it was an occasion if we heard a tractor coming, all the boys in particular would all flock down to the wire fence at the bottom and cling on to the chain link fence and peer out over to see who it was. If it was a strange vehicle it would be an event. I remember a chap called Gerald Brommel used to come around, I think it was Tuesdays and Thursdays, with a baker's van. If we could we'd take a threepenny bit to buy a cream doughnut off him. Unless he got to school at breaktime, we'd miss our doughnut because Mrs Stevens wouldn't let us go out to get it. On an odd occasion for a special treat we might, but generally if Gerald didn't come on time, we wouldn't get our doughnut.

On the first of July 1949 we went to Bristol Zoo and that was a real day out! We went by train from Bideford Station."

The first intimation that the school might be closed came in 1946 and although it was to be another twelve years before this happened, it was the beginning of the end.

November 26th 1946. At a Special Meeting of the Managers.
This meeting was called for the purpose of considering a letter from the County, suggesting the closure of the School and transferring the children to Bideford. After careful consideration the Correspondent was directed to reply that the Managers were strongly opposed to this proposal because it would be very hard on the children and probably injurious to their health having such a long day as this proposal would entail. Other reasons were: (1) There would be transport difficulties in this scattered area, (2) the school is part and parcel of the village and to lose it would be a big loss to the social life of the village, (3) the premises are second to none in the district and admirably suited to the school use.
13th September 1948.
A Special Meeting was called for the purpose of considering the County's proposal to close the School. It was decided to organise a parish petition and protest to the Ministry against this step.

2nd October 1957.

The meeting was called to meet members of the Divisional Education Committee. It was intimated that a proposal would be made shortly to close Littleham School and transfer the children to Bideford.

9th May 1958.

It was reported that a petition organised by the Parish Council, signed by practically all the inhabitants of the Parish, had been forwarded to the Minister of Education protesting at the proposed closing of the School.

The petition was unsuccessful. The final decision to close the school was received during the summer holidays and the children started the new term at Bideford schools, deprived even of the chance to say goodbye to the school which had served the parish for eighty one years. Many people feel that this was the major cause of the decline of Littleham as a community, that the heart of the village had been ripped out. A few however felt the children would benefit from attending a bigger school.

"At the end, Mrs Stevens was unwell and when she was unwell there'd be a relief teacher and it was most difficult. It was children from five to eleven, sixteen children, and everybody was really very much against closing the village school but we felt, well they wouldn't replace Mrs Stevens and we felt it wasn't very satisfactory. To us, taking children into town and that brand new school, we thought it was to their advantage because it was too quiet an environment in Littleham. I couldn't take them anywhere because I didn't drive. But I don't think many agree with us! Now we could do with another school really."

Certainly there are enough children in the village now but it is quite unknown for a new village school to open these days and the pressures on such schools since the advent of the Education Reform Act are such that it would no longer be desirable to do so. But there is no doubt that the village has suffered as a community since the closure. Winifred Johns is aware of the change.

"Children was much more friendly in they days. Now I maintain that's because there's no village school. I know we're older but they're not friendly like they used to be when they were at the village school. This has been an open door for children ever since we've been here. I don't believe kids today can go into conversation, whether it's the television or what I don't know but they are different. That school should never have closed."

Chapter Fifteen

Lanes and Dwellings

During the last thirty years the number of houses in Littleham has doubled from approximately forty-five to ninety, drastically altering the appearance of the village as well as causing considerable change to the social fabric. The rate at which Littleham has expanded is typical of most villages in North Devon and most of the new houses are unfortunately also typical for their lack of harmony with the surrounding landscape. It is difficult to imagine the village now without the new houses, difficult to remember how it was even ten years ago when walking through the village was a walk along a country lane, the high hedgebanks only occasionally interrupted by houses. How much more noticeable must the changes be to those such as Charlie who have lived all their lives in the village.

"I went to Westleigh, well the things that had altered, I didn't know where I was out there! I couldn't find the village hall at all, I didn't know where I was at all, there's so many houses being built around there. You wouldn't think you'd lose yourself like that, would 'ee? I think if some of these old people were to come back yer now, they wouldn't know where the hell they was. If you took all the new houses away there'd be nothing yer would there! You can hardly think that there was so many children up here at the school can you?"

Many of the older buildings have changed too, in their usage and sometimes also in external appearance. Most of the cottages in Mount Pleasant were rented rather than owner-occupied, all were originally thatched and now have slate roofs, the same is true of several farmhouses. Two cottages which were originally one up, one down have been incorporated with adjoining properties. Ten new properties have been created from barns and derelict buildings, including the old school which having been used to house chickens for some years had become progressively more dilapidated, it has now been beautifully renovated retaining all the original architectural features. Hoops Cottage, a pretty stone and cob cottage with leaded windows on the outskirts of the village, was the pub until about 1930 but few memories of it remain.

"I wasn't old enough to drink when that pub was there, Hoop Inn, that was the one opposite to where it is now. But coming back that way one day with my father from somewhere or other, 'e wanted a drink and 'e said, you coming een? He said you can have a drop of pop if you like. So I went in once that I remember and had a glass of pop and he had a glass of beer, the old landlord was called Jenkins then."

"There was a pub in the village but Gilbert was only a tea boy when they were taking water from Melbury Reservoir out to Jennetts and he was only, well he'd only just left school, fourteen I suppose. And the men used to send him up to Littleham to opposite the Crealock, there was a pub there, Hoop Inn. Gilbert can remember going in there and bringing back a can of beer for the men that was working, he was too young to drink so what he had I don't know, I daresay he had a drop!"

Sylventray, one of the newer houses in the village with a very large, well kept garden has interesting origins. The site was bought by gypsies who eventually replaced their caravan with a pre-fab, after being sold this was extended and improved to create the present house.

"There were gypsies in the village. Mr Birch used to be up the lane quite a lot, Apps Lane, he was always up the lane in the way of my Granfer and my Granfer said to him, you clear off and he said I will if you sell me that field and he sold him the field for a hundred pound! Today it'd be worth a lot, probably then he was glad to be rid of something, I don't know. But he was rather a nice man, Birch was. He pulled the caravan in there and put four posts around it, real gypsy caravan."

The original use of the Old Forge, now a beautifully kept house with smart white outbuildings, is evident. William, now aged ninety, was able to relate a story about the forge which was painful enough to have been remembered since the middle of the last century. "Oh yes, the blacksmiths shop. When you had a toothache you'd go to the blacksmiths shop to have a tooth pulled! I've heard my grandparents talk about that!" Charlie also remembered the forge being in use.

"The forge? Yes, Dennis he was called, he used to be a bell-ringer too. He used to shoe horses and all that down there. He always used to smoke and when it got the end of the cigarette, when it got very small he used to push a nail in to have the last whiff! Very queer, 'tis funny how you remember these things! Course us was children then and us used to have a laugh about it. We used to like to see him hitting and the sparks flying and shoeing horses, 'twas marvellous really, have the old hot shoe and put it right on the foot and 'twould steam. You'd think it would hurt the horses but still it didn't. He'd do any implements, you know, like ploughs and that on the farm."

By the forties, there was not enough trade for the forge to operate every day. Vi McDougall:

"I can't remember the blacksmiths shop being open every day, Georgie Copp used to come over from Parkham twice a week, Wednesdays and Fridays I think it was. Of course there were still quite a lot of horses working on the land so he was quite busy. It was always quite enjoyable to go up there, people used to forgather there like anything, almost like going to the pub because I suppose they got Parkham news as well as exchanging Littleham news. Then in the cold weather it was nice and cosy in there. Sometimes the horses were a bit tiresome and Georgie used to cuss at them a bit and I remember Mrs Atkinson at Crossways saying that he'd apologised one day and said perhaps she'd heard him "talking"! He used to repair all the farm machinery, you used to go there and there'd be harrows that he used to call drags, he used to repoint the bit that went into the ground, anything like that he did. There was very little waiting room, there was a very small shed which took one or two ponies, otherwise you had to wait out in the open which was rather tiresome on a nasty day."

The village hall is a long low building situated a quarter of a mile from the centre of Littleham, it is notoriously difficult for visitors to find as they invariably turn back before reaching it, not believing that it can still be ahead when the village has been left behind. Its position was not chosen deliberately, first attempts to build on glebe land next to the church were foiled and the present site was rented from Captain Bell of Heale House for a peppercorn rent. Unfortunately the lease of the land was not made legally tenable, this caused considerable problems after Captain Bell's death and took several years to resolve. William is probably the only person still alive who helped to build the original hall in 1910.

"I remember it being built, we started building it down opposite the back church gate and we got the walls about this high and they suddenly found that it was on glebe land and it wasn't allowed so we had to cart all the bricks again up to the crossway and built up there. It was built as a rifle range, a shooting gallery. Well of course it's been extended since then."

A skittle alley was added in 1924 but old habits die hard.

"The parish hall was built as a rifle range and the old people still called it the rifle range, talk about the parish hall, oh no it was the rifle range."

Winifred Johns first started using the hall in the thirties. Her memories are not all pleasant.

"'Twas always the rifle range and 'twasn't going to be anything else for the older people. 'Twas a horrible little hall really when I first went there. There was a coalhouse out where the toilets is now and there was a furnace and you had to light that one underneath with the tap coming through the wall for your water. Well needless to say we didn't do much of that, not the W.I., we brought kettles and boiled them on the fire.

The water was fetched from Apps Farm so you only used what was necessary. It was cold, one fire for the whole of the place. Later years they built that bar out the other end, well the W.I. bought oil stoves, Alladin lamps, and heated up with that and tried to make it a bit more comfortable. Until in the end you see we were doing so much, buying cups and saucers and all this sort of thing and someone said, well who does it belong to, who are we doing it for and then of course they started sifting into it and it didn't really belong to the village and it was an awful to do for a long time before they could get it settled up."

The hall has been steadily improved over the years and plans now exist for a further extension.

Apps Farm has seen many changes of fortune over the years. A brewery was established in about 1850 and it must have been at this time that the massive stone buildings surrounding the old farmhouse were built. It was an ideal site for a brewery, there being an apparently limitless supply of spring water and several large wells were sunk in the area. Beer and mineral water was bottled and seems to have been produced in great quantities, certainly it achieved sufficient recognition to be mentioned in Harrods Royal County Directory of Devonshire for 1878.

"This place is noted for brewing the 'Apps ale' which, according to analytical chemists, possesses medical properties of the most valuable nature, and is particularly adapted for invalids and others of weak digestion."

If these claims were true, the people of Littleham must have been a healthy bunch.

"The men at the Brewery, I've heard say their allowance was a gallon a day and so if one was a teetotaller the other one had the beer!"

The fortunes of the brewery took a turn for the worse in 1885 when a serious fire destroyed many of the buildings and much valuable equipment. It was reported by the Bideford Gazette on 17th March 1885.

"DISASTEROUS FIRE NEAR BIDEFORD

Apps Brewery Burnt Down

On Sunday morning a fire occurred which was of a far more serious nature than any which has taken place in Bideford or in the neighbourhood for many years past. The scene of the conflagration was App's Brewery, about two miles from the town, and its result was the burning to the ground of nearly the whole of the premises constituting this well known brewery. In fact the whole of the brewery proper was burnt; the malting houses and a few sheds, which were detached, being all that escaped...The fire, however, even when discovered, had already a hold on the building, and the flames spread with a rapidity and the fire burnt with a ferocity which was simply frightful."

The article goes on to state that as soon as the fire was noticed, a man galloped off to Bideford to raise the alarm.

"The messenger left the Brewery at 9.30 a.m. and it was about ten minutes to ten when the news reached Bideford and by the time the hour had struck the men had been called together, the engine got out, the horses brought down from the New Inn stables, and a start effected. Apps was reached about the half hour, and the engine was speedily got to work. The supply of water was plentiful, and the services of the engine proved most useful. By this time, however, the whole of the brewery was nearly gutted....

We have said that the origin of the fire is mysterious. Not only was the outbreak very sudden, and at, so to speak, an unlikely time, but nothing is known which can be supposed to in any way have caused it... It is not likely the amount of insurance will cover the loss... The total damage cannot yet be estimated, but it must amount to several thousand pounds. We are authorised to add that Mr Philbrick has decided to re-erect the premises without delay, and that he has arranged to carry on his business as usual in the meantime.

Some hundreds of people were present whilst the fire was raging, and on Sunday afternoon and yesterday the spot was visited by several hundreds more."

It seems that a certain amount of refurbishment took place because the brewery continued in business until the turn of the century but it must have been in a reduced form as the buildings were never replaced. The massive barns which remain formed but a small part of the brewery as it was until the fire. A more recent owner found signs of the fire.

"That big building behind the cottage was more of a store place for the Brewery. The buildings for the Brewery used to go right up through the yard and that was where the fire was so that part was knocked down. When we were decorating the farmhouse we found scorch marks, the beams had been burnt. That was on the left as you look at the porch. Father used to say, oh there was a big fire here and 'twasn't insured but it was before his time."

When the brewery ceased trading, Apps was sold and reverted to a farm but it was recognized that the remaining buildings had potential beyond that of simple farm use and before long a slaughterhouse was in business.

"Course my Granfer had a slaughterhouse at Apps. He used to kill about a hundred lamb a day. He was always up at five o'clock every morning and sometimes before because he had to go to market and buy and not now like these days when you get there in half an hour, he had to travel a long way. So he used to get up at five o'clock and walk the farm and see the sheep and then have his breakfast then he would be on the move with the pony and trap by nine o'clock, he would get to market by eleven o'clock. He'd buy from the market and he'd have a drover and what he bought, the drover would bring them back. And the dogs in those days were wonderful dogs, more rougher, bark more, a rougher type of dog more like an Old English Sheepdog, stand at the back of the flock and bark. They would drive sheep from Stibb Cross, Hartland. When I was a boy, that was for Father, we would go to Stibb Cross market and have to walk them home. They would be slaughtered then taken by wagon to the station. There was Granfer working there and Father and his brother and two men and a drover. The slaughterhouse was where they've got the two bungalows now, it was a smaller building than what you would think, for hanging a hundred sheep it didn't need a big area."

Apps Farm has now undergone another change of use. The farm-house, cottage and outbuidings have been sold and the barns and outbuildings converted to seven dwellings. The whole will be sufficiently large to form a hamlet quite seperate from the main village but its future is as yet dependent on the vicissitudes of the property market.

There is one more story attached to Apps. It seems that for a short time after the brewery closed there was a tenant who entertained a rather unusual guest.

"There was a bear over at Apps! Us used to go over and look at it through the bars, where the stable is now, just round the corner as you go in the gate. You'd look in there and he'd be looking out! Standing up, catching hold the bars! Then we'd see him out on a rope and the man would have a great big stick, he'd be walking along on his back legs like a man! I don't think I've ever seen him on his four legs. But I know it was a lovely thing, lovely white fur on him, what they'd call a polar bear I suppose."

An albino Brown Bear, in retirement after years of dancing at a fair perhaps? But life is hard for the oral historian, and the truth not always easy to pin down.

"A bear? 'Twas wolves! My father used to go past Apps going to school and they used to go in to terrify the wolves. He used to say it was wolves. There was always the iron bars there on the stable on the left as you go in. I can mind my father talking about it, I used to say, what's they bars there for and he used to say, oh they used to have wolves in yer."

Recollections of things actually seen by the speaker are probably more reliable than memories which are passed down through the generations. Some things however are not immutable, events can be interpretated in different ways according to the viewpoint of the individual concerned, the passage of time may lead things to be seen in a different, and often rosier, light. Just as facts become altered as they are passed on by word of mouth, so names undergo subtle transformations over the years, as if communicated in a centuries long game of Chinese whispers. Field names are rarely used now except by the farmers themselves but in the past everyone in the village would have known the name of each field as they would either work on the land themselves or have a very close relation who did so. Names were needed not only to refer to fields that needed to be worked but also by those who used them as shortcuts and for recreational purposes. Public access to farmland was not the issue it has become today. It was not usually prohibited when farming was less intensive and damage therefore less likely to occur, and when everyone in the locality had a close association with and understanding of farming. The tithe map of 1841 shows field names in use at the time which had no doubt undergone subtle changes over the years. When I talked to Charlie Cook I found there had been further changes in the common usage of names.

"The field over here (East Above Town on 1841 map) is Budown, I don't know exactly how to spell it, whether it's Budown or Butown, I think it's Budown. This field next to me where the houses is now was Moory Meadow. The one in front of the school was Centrely (Sanctuary on 1841 map), I don't know why it was called that, it seems queer! The children from Edge Mills used to come up that way to the school. Then the field below the church is Path Meadow, (Best Meadow). This lane out here was called Watery Lane, no traffic ever went down here because it was just water and stones, no road like there is now, a few people perhaps would walk down there if they could get between the stones! So that's Watery Lane!

The field down below the pond, that used to be two. They dug down the hedge parting the two, the second one was called Bumpy Meadow, (Cross Park on 1841 map). The two belonged to two different persons you see, one in each farm. I've walked down there a time, that lane down there used to go down by Edge Mills, you could walk right down through there, I've done that scores of times, well it's filled in now i'n'it, it's filled in, the lane, I forgot that. All these old places were very nice, the times I used to go down there, when I was a kid we'd go down there and climb up the trees! You could go in any of the fields, no one used to say anything to 'ee. 'Tis different now, I suppose it's right enough in a way, it's somebody walking on your property after all but I don't know, everybody seemed to be equal somehow, all in one sort of, you can do this, you can do what you like!"

There are numerous examples of tracks which have disappeared over the years, either through disuse or through the need to create more productive land. In the lane which approaches the old school an old gateway can be seen, overgrown now with brambles and apparently giving access only to an area of trees and dense undergrowth but another old inhabitant recalled its original use.

"Have you seen that old gateway on the right before you get to the Old School? That was the front drive to the Rectory. Oh it was a lovely drive, lovely with primroses. That lane we go down now, that was just a little track, the main drive was for carriages. We weren't supposed to go down that way really but we did, used to love to run down that drive. It had a lovely back garden, where the car park is now was the vegetable garden with greenhouses, there used to be a cottage there to but I don't remember anyone living there. That's where the British Legion went right after the first war."

It is easy to assume that modern innovations always mean improvements in physical conditions but this is not always so. I had assumed that before roads were tarmac, they were merely muddy tracks which would have been difficult to negotiate in winter but the truth proved to be very different. When labour was cheap it was possible for much time to be spent on the upkeep of roads.

"The roads were a lot cleaner than what they be today, 'tis awful today! No gutters to take the water away see, they used to be out with their long-handled shovels clearing the gutters right down through, water'd be running down gutters instead of out in the road. Years ago they used to crack stones and roll them in, it wasn't muddy 'cause the water was runnin' down the gutters out the way. There used to be a stone depot by the phone box there, I've seen them in there a time, there cracking stone. You see where those houses is, there was a deep quarry, just below, when they was building in there I said, well I'm damned if I know, there's a master big quarry in there. Course they filled it up I know, years ago, but even then, it may cause to sink. Yep, you could drive a horse and cart right in there, they used to blow with dynamite in there an' all. The stone was put down on the roads mostly."

"One of the things that's the worst, very much worse, is that in those days for years George Brend and Edgar used to go around and clean the ditches in the lanes and they used to go round and round doing it and so the lanes were so much better even though you did have cows toddling up and down. It seems to me that the fields are much wetter and I'm sure it is because the water just goes down the lane and into the field, it used to go down the ditches."

In ninety years, William has seen many changes both in the appearance and use of the roads.

"Our back lane here, that was the way people used to walk to Bideford. There was just room for a carriage, hardly room enough for a tractor, it's a difficult job now to trim the hedge with a tractor really. It all improved as time went on you see, when they only wanted a walking space, then that was all they made, now you see it's motor carriageways all to meet up with the expansion in every way. Time doesn't stand still, people are always studying something whether it's better or not. All the roads were like that, stones were put down and they'd go in in their time, it depended how small they were cracked down to. There used to be quite a number of stone depots about where they would crack the stones, a man would be there with a hammer cracking the stones. There was one opposite Apps, there's a run in at the top of the track there, well that used to be a stone depot. They used to cart all the stones in there and a man would be in there hammering away, breaking the stones. Tarmacking didn't come for quite a while and some were never tarmacked, our back lane and Mark's Lane, that used to be the main way to Bideford at one time. I imagine they went out and went down to Upcott Hill."

The lower section of Wagon Road where it joins the A386 was built for the wagons from the brewery, the existing lanes being too steep for such large vehicles.

"You do hear 'em say that there was only Upcott Hills and you had to pay a toll to come up Wagon Road one time. I have heard Father say, no there wasn't no Wagon Road, not before the Brewery came. Why they made it so zig-zaggy was so it wasn't quite so steep for the horses."

Some commodities in the village have been lost through disuse. The village pump was swallowed up by new housing despite pleas to to retain it as an attractive feature, it would have been useful too in recent summers when there have been water restrictions. The village pond is now merely a grassy depression with one muddy corner despite attempts to restore it, it could have considerable aesthetic appeal but the original need for it has now disappeared.

"The pond's always been there, all the cattle used to go there as they came up from the fields, they'd go over there and drink every time. There was a lot of grass growing all up around it, there was only just room for the cows to go in and drink. Then when it was thrashing up that farm, they used to come down there and put water in their engines from there."

There was a shop in Littleham until 1987. There have been intervals in the past when the village was without a shop but it seems unlikely that another will open now that the car provides easy access to the town and few people are willing to put in long hours for small renumeration. Charlie remembered how the site of the shop changed over the years.

"There was a shop once there where you used to live, next door to where you are now, there was a shop down opposite the pub, used to be the old pub, and next door to where I used to live, where Johnny

Devereux is now, they used to sell a few things there; but not all at once, you know when one finished perhaps somebody else would take on and it was not constant sort of thing because if the one person who'd got the shop stopped, well that would be it until somebody else made up their minds to do a bit of it see. It was cigarettes mostly they used to sell. Mrs Badcock of course had the Post Office, that was the first one as far as I can remember. Then of course it went down Langdon way, they didn't stop there very long."

Gertie Beer recalled that not all the shopkeepers were equally popular.

"There were two shops when I was at school (1905-1914). There was a Miss Kivell and a Miss Martin, she was right opposite the school, she had a sweet shop. Miss Kivell was an old maid and she used to look after us children when Father and Mother used to go out, they used to go out to see their parents. She used to have a sweet shop in the village next to where you are, Miss Kivell used to and Miss Martin, she was more generous, she used to give you a few over and we got used to that you see. So one day I was there and Miss Kivell was there and I said, oh, I want to go out, I've got some pocket money. And I was foolish enough to say oh, I want a few sweets. Oh, her said, I can sell you a few sweets and she used to count them out you know! I wanted the most I could get!"

It is difficult to see how the village will grow and change in the future. There are still many sites within the boundary on which building could take place and it may be that within a few years many more areas will be under concrete. Much depends on the state of the property market which having expanded so rapidly during the eighties, is now at a standstill. Will there be any stories to relate about Littleham in a hundred years time? In a dormitory village, life seems to take place elsewhere.

Chapter Sixteen

The Village Today

There can be few people who would want to carry all their water from the village pump again, to work such long hours for little money, to walk to town and return with heavy shopping. But all the older inhabitants of Littleham missed the sense of belonging they used to feel, of everyone knowing each other and sharing common experiences. This comradeship has gone and its passing is felt as a great loss. No one I spoke to had anything good to say about the newcomers to the village and it sometimes seems that there is an undeclared war between the two factions. In the interests of future harmony, it will be as well not to mention any names in this chapter lest this book be used as a further weapon in the conflict.

"When you moved in, you moved in and wanted to be a part of the village didn't 'ee whereas ones that moved in since don't want to be part of the village. They want to live in the country, they want a nice view but they don't want country life and after a couple of years they move on."

It does seem that some of the newcomers believe the surrounding countryside is for their enjoyment, it must be picturesque and accessible. This leads to conflict with farmers over such issues as new barns being erected which are not as attractive as old stone-built barns, and access to farmland by establishing public footpaths which farmers want to avoid at all costs, being wary of damaged crops and straying cattle.

"A lot of these people who come out of the towns want the amenities of a town life but the quietness of a country life, see? Well you can't have the both. People come yer and they want to change things, why do they come yer in the first place? If these people had their way with these right of ways, how they was gwain on, you could say every field in Littleham was a right of way because in the past you could walk where you liked and nobody stopped you. It wasn't like it is now, we all knew each other. They wouldn't think to stop you, you wouldn't think to ask, you knew everybody and you trusted everybody. People didn't go round leaving gates open for the cattle and things like that. From the time I can remember to the time I left my first cottage, we never locked the front door. We'd go to Westward Ho! of a Sunday and the front door would be left open, you knaw, 'e'd be left unlocked. You can hardly go up to post a letter now without locking the door."

Because locals and newcomers have not had time to get to know each other, both groups tend to see each other in the form of stereotypes which although perhaps containing a grain of truth, are greatly exaggerated; newcomers are ignorant of farming and will leave gates open wherever they go; farmers are anti-conservationist, power-hungry, out to make big profits at the expense of "nature". These differences are masked by a veneer of politeness which may lead everyone to believe that all is going smoothly but if challenged, as happened recently when the newcomers formed a committee to ask for new public footpaths, the mask is quickly dropped and the population is polarised into two distinct groups. Some believe the problem will get worse rather than better.

"You see what's going to happen in years to come, all these barns being converted and the people that's buying these sorts of places are out of towns so therefore when the farmer hisself's got his cows there and they're shouting and bawling all night long, people in the houses gwain to start complaining about that, they're going to start complaining about the smell, they're going to complain about the muck and one thing and another and when these young farmers come up there'll be no, there won't be any houses left to farm on, no barns or sheds. It's Littleham's downfall that the council, the parish council have allowed it. This is the point, they haven't tried to stop it."

There is no doubt that things have changed for farmers. They have lost the considerable authority they held as employers when a large percentage of the village population was in their employ. It is worth remembering that social change in the village and the influx of people from towns has been provoked by changes in agriculture. Over the years many former labourers have been forced to leave villages to find work as farming became increasingly mechanised and it may be that some villages would have become deserted if people had not moved in from the towns. It does seem that some farmers are unwilling to relinquish their former power and in the struggle to regain it, they may find it is not only the newcomers who resent them.

"Years ago we had an open meeting, they'd been round with a petition to clean the village up. At the time I was chairman of the Parish Hall Committee, I signed my name to it, I *would* like to see the village cleaned up. And when I came out of the open meeting I had a lot of farmers saying, you're chairman of the committee, you should keep your mouth shut, and you work down Orleigh Mills and we're your bread and butter. And I said, well do you know, from '39 to '45 there was a bloke called Hitler went around telling people what to do like and I said you're doing the same. I said I had three years in the airforce, just 'cause you're farmers you haven't got to do nothing. Well, they said, seeing where you work to, you should keep your mouth shut. I said well when the likes of you tell me I got to keep my mouth shut, I might as well be down the churchyard 'cause I ain't any good to meself or anybody else."

A common criticism of the newcomers is their supposed sense of superiority.

"I honestly think that some of these who come down from the Home Counties, they think the straw's still growing out from under our hats. There's a superior feeling about it though they're not all like it of course. It's a great pity they don't integrate readily but there it is, I think it's going to take several decades if not a couple of generations and of course they won't stay that long. I don't think Littleham the only place that's suffering from this problem. Sadly it does destroy the village life and the school's gone, that at least would have been a focal point.

In the past the average person looked up to Major Atkinson and he was a genuine, nice ex-military chap, you know, a perfect gentleman. I suppose it's not right to use the expression that some people are jumped up, they move in and they - I suppose it's partly that so many people have become so materialistic really. I just don't know, I haven't got any kids and it's not for me to say really but I hear all sorts of stories around. When we were kids we made our own fun, now some of the kids in the village, they haven't got time to mix within the community, they're whisked away to play tennis or whisked away to go swimming, they're driven around with their parents all the time whereas in our young day the only thing we had was bicycles or you had to walk. And of course as soon as everything is slowed down you tend to meet people because people are going along at a lesser speed all the time. Now a car goes through the village and it's gone. It's a great pity but I'm afraid it's just one of these things, I just don't see any answer to it."

Class differences tend to be widened because each group is using different criteria to judge the other. A farm labourer who gained status through being a good worker finds he is judged by the newcomers by his education and material possessions. The newcomers are unaware of the status gained through working for the same employer for many years, through reliability and "knowing all there is to know" about the job. To them such a worker seems lacking in ambition, incapable of progress. The locals retaliate in the only way they are able, accusing the newcomers of ignorance of the locality so that the length of stay becomes a sign of status.

"The people who we've had come in the last two year, most of them think you're ignorant and they think just because you've lived out in the country all your life that you don't know nothing and they try to take the mickey out of 'ee and try to make 'ee look a laughing stock. The village isn't like it used to be, nothing like, not even when you come here first. There's not a village atmosphere anymore, it's, you know, one against the other. It takes a long time for people like us to accept somebody but once you do you're a friend for life sort of thing you know. People who move in now, they want to take over everything but they don't want to do nothing. They say, we want so and so but they don't want to help with nothing. I'm not helping with the fete this year, this is the first year I've never helped with the fete since it's been going, thirty two year, and *he* said well why not? I said for the simple reason that last year we was up there, it was half past four and somebody came to us and said, have you had a cup of tea yet? No. Have anybody been to relieve 'ee? I said no. And there was his folks that was on the committee walking around doing nothing. Ah well, he said, they've never seen a fete before. Well I said, if they've never seen a fete before, I said they work at their own and they go to Buckland, they go to Monkleigh, they go to Weare Gifford, that's where they see the fetes, I said they don't do it at their own. He said so you aren't helping, I said no, I idn't."

It is difficult to know what the newcomers could do to improve relations except perhaps just stay put and wait for the dust to settle. They might just find that they are accepted as long-term residents when it is all over. Certainly it does not help to try to do too much but it is difficult to find the balance, newcomers tend to be accused either of having no interest in the village or of wanting to take over. One person I spoke to was somewhat bemused by her reception.

"I have to say I have found it much harder to get to know the locals here than in other places I have lived; I have lived in the country before and have been accepted immediately as part of the community. It may be because North Devon has been fairly isolated in the past, I don't know, but I find I'm regarded with great suspicion and it sometimes seems that whatever I say or do upsets somebody. It's rather like trying to play a game when no one will tell you the rules."

Many of the older inhabitants still wave or smile at passing cars and certainly always greet anyone on foot, it seems a simple politeness and it is after all only a few years since everyone who passed was well known. This is an obvious cause of friction when the greeting is not returned, especially when two cars meet on the narrow lanes and protocol is not observed.

"We used to know everyone in the village, we used to speak to everyone we met. Now it's not quite the same is it? We'd say good morning to everyone or a smile or something but we don't get that anymore, that's what we miss rather. We find now people don't like backing for you and things like that, they look evil at you, whereas in our day it was always hello Bill or hello Tom and if you had to go back well you always reckoned to give them a smile. I don't think people can back p'raps, that's the first thing I had to learn, if you can't back, ain't much point in learning to drive! In the olden days you could fall out with someone today and forget it tomorrow. We won't never see the old village again, nothing don't go back."

The newcomer can easily earn a reputation for obstinancy and rudeness if he does not immediately reverse his car to let another pass; it is the simple rule that whoever is nearest a passing place should reverse but of course this is difficult to judge until the lanes are well known, and by then enmity may already have formed.

Perhaps a distorted picture is formed through talking to the older residents. It is only when a dispute arises over a certain issue that the polarities of the two camps becomes clear, otherwise life goes on peacefully enough; Littleham is still a very pleasant place to live. It is probable that the dilemma will be solved with the passing of time although it is more likely that the newcomers will form a new community than learn the rules of what remains of the existing one. Some of the older people have died, others have become disillusioned with the changing village and have moved to neighbouring towns.

"It all used to be one big happy family, didn't it. The village was just a few families, 'twas the Beers and the Badcocks and the Cooks and the Uptons. Now it's grown so and all the older ones has gone on, the family atmosphere went. I wouldn't go back although I've lived there all my life."

Several families who have lived in the village all their lives have now moved out and more may follow for a variety of reasons.

"If we go it'll be because it's too big for us here, we don't want the work now. But that's the only reason we'd go. There again there's money in bricks and mortar and if you think, well that's the only way you're going to have a little bit extra you know. I think some people are thinking about their old age when they move, perhaps when they wouldn't be able to drive a car, if only someone was able to make a living like they used to out of the shop and the post office you could be sure you wouldn't need a car in your old age."

There is no doubt that the new community will be very different from the old. The neighbourliness of the past was essential when everyone was in such close and frequent contact; now that work and leisure pursuits take place outside the village the opportunities for getting to know fellow villagers are limited. The newcomer to the area may find herself in a particularly difficult position, having imagined perhaps that village life will provide an instant community with plenty of potential friends, she may find instead that she belongs neither to the town nor the village.

The small villages of North Devon may have been physically isolated in the past but they are far more isolating for the individual today, a disappointment no doubt to many new arrivals. People do still want to feel a part of a community and organizations and committees are set up in an attempt to recreate the sense of togetherness which used to arise naturally through living and working together. The need for such organizations may be questioned:

"They've got these ideas now for improving the village hall, all right it do need improving but is the villagers going to use it? Cos they don't. Tony's the only Littleham man in the skittles A team, the others have all moved out now and just come back to play. The bingo, 'tis all outsiders, there's only a handful of Littleham people. I can't see it's going to be used anymore when the work's done."

There is no doubt however that much can be achieved, a thriving youth club has been established and a considerable amount of money raised for the replacement of the church bells, both immediately benefitting the village. It may be that this will be the future of village life, a rather artificial society of disparate individuals who have come together in an attempt to create a sense of belonging.

There are other possibilities. Village communities have changed largely because the inhabitants have to leave the village to work. If work could again be found in the village, through choice rather than necessity, there would be hope for the community of the future. This may not be as unlikely as it sounds. More and more people throughout the country are choosing to work at home either on their own or linked to large offices by computer and their numbers seem likely to increase. There is already a nursery, small workshop, two garages, a market garden and two carpenter's workshops in Littleham. There is a painter and decorator and two builders who work largely in the village. There are artists, craftsmen and a writer working at home. There are people at home caring for young children, retired people, disabled and house-bound people. If these numbers were to increase over the next few years there would again be a need for a village shop and post office, villagers would again meet naturally as they went about their work and daily chores. It could be a community which retained the advantages of the old way of life without the disadvantages. Vain hopes perhaps, but the need for a sense of belonging in an ever more fragmented world is strong. Who knows what might be achieved?